Tusquittee Tales:
Stories That Made the Water Dogs Laugh

Tusquittee Tales:
Stories That Made the Water Dogs Laugh

Howard Blankenship

ISBN 978-1-300-20612-5

Foreword

Howard first came into my life in the fall of 2011. I passed by a pasture while driving down Cold Branch Road and saw a horse standing parallel to the fence, head up, perfectly still. When I drove by later in the day, it was still there, in the same spot. Although I didn't know much about horse behavior, I found this odd, so I backed up and pulled in to check it out.

The horse had on a halter with a clip and somehow managed to clip itself to the fence. I unhooked him, took the halter off, looked around and saw nothing in the way of food although there was plenty of fresh water provided by a stream. I looked across and down the road and saw a barn full of hay. I headed that way and ended up at Howard's family homestead. Howard's mom, Muriel answered the door, said she was expecting Howard shortly, and she would send him down.

That afternoon, Howard showed up at the pasture with a bale of hay and some feed. I discovered that the horse had an owner that was temporarily out of town. We decided it would be best to leave his halter off so he couldn't clip himself again. When we got back to his house, I noticed three more horses looking wistfully over a cattle fence on property across the street. Howard had been providing hay for these over the last winter. One of the horses was a dainty looking mare that I instantly fell in love with. I asked Howard to find out if the owner wanted to sell her.

Howard is nothing if not gregarious, and I got to hear quite a few entertaining tales about growing up in the Tusquittee Mountain Valley while we tended to the horses over the next few days. I mentioned that he ought to write a book, and he said "Well, I am!"

Turns out he has a laptop PC that he taught himself to use and he had written page after page about family, friends and adventures while growing up in the Cold Branch area.

After reading a few, I offered to edit them for him. He gave me printed copies to take back home and start work on. A couple of weeks later I get a phone call from Howard, telling me that I am now the proud owner of Daisy, the chestnut mare. He had traded hay for her and moved her over to his property which has a barn, a fresh stream and all the hay she wants. Daisy Mae is now quite a fine looking horse, and stays busy "mowing" Howard's pastures until I can get her down to Florida. Or, if I'm really lucky, until I can spend much of my time up there!

This is the Tusquittee way—Howard's way—of sharing in life, of trading one thing for another; where one kindness is repaid a hundredfold and a good(or bad) deed always comes back around.

I decided I would leave the stories just as Howard had written them, simply dividing his stream of consciousness style of writing into book format. Howard's voice and personality come through loud and clear! I am sure you will find him as entertaining and likable as I do. His positive outlook on life is infectious; he likes to "look at the sunny side of the grass," and when you ask him how he is, he always says "If I were any better I'd have to be twins!"

Howard's stories are funny, some a little off-color, and some come across a bit righteous, but they are all from the heart. They are stories about life and people in the Tusquittee Mountain region of Cold Branch. They show us that every day can be rich in family, friends, adventures and living life to the fullest. I feel blessed to know Howard and to have a hand in bringing this book to you.
Enjoy!

Maddie Lock
Editor

Contents

The Circle ~ May it Never be Broken

Back in the early '70s, a group of people got together, and little did we know what was going to be taking place. It was Christmas time, and everyone likes a party, so we the group got up a Christmas party. It was to take place on Chairmaker Branch just off Nelson Ridge road.

Well, us guys, we all were to meet at the chosen place, and build a shelter to have the party in. That Friday, about six of us arrived at noon and built a shack of sorts. We made it about 20' by 20', and wrapped it in plastic, then put in an old barrel for a stove, and cut a lot of fire wood, because this get together was to last through the holidays.

At 4:00 in the afternoon the people started to arrive, and as they walked into the shanty they would open up their coolers and start hanging great big buds on the wall for Christmas decorations, and on the table they sat all sorts of different spirits. Everyone had their own recipe of moonshine and the buds were of every type and strain.

By 7:00 the party was in full swing, and as people kept coming, the wilder the party got. By Saturday night it was getting pretty wild. They was about 60 people and more coming as the night went on. By the time Sunday morning rolled around, they was people laying all over the ground. Some were even in the trees. We even had one walking in the coals of the fire!

When Sunday evening came around, the folks started to thin out some, because some of them had jobs. By Monday morning we had shut the party down until the following Friday. That way we could rest up a little bit and bring in the New Year in style.

Friday rolled around and the party started again. This time, they were a whole lot less folks there, and we were glad, because things did get a little out of hand and the law found out about it. By Sunday afternoon we were having a good old time, and here come someone with the Forest Service, and trouble.

This guy, he didn't have a sense of humor at all. He asked what we were doing and we said that we had a little party, and were minding our own business and he should mind his own. Well, this didn't go over too good, needless to say, so he starts checking folks for firearms, and as usual everyone had one. Everyone carried one them days just to kill snakes and skunks.

This officer, he said that he would have to relieve us of our guns, but no one would give theirs up; we told him to get his own. At this, he started to get mad and he went to his truck and got on his radio to call for help. Well, everyone walked to their cars, got in and drove off. All the while he was trying to stop us.

Well, this officer, he never got a name or a tag number, and as we were going down the road, out of a side road pulls a deputy sheriff car. But when he seen us all coming down that gravel road as fast as we could hold it in the road, he got out of the way real fast. By the time everything shook out, nobody was caught and no one got a ticket.

After this incident we were very careful to have our parties in different spots and never in the same place twice. This prompted us to form a circle of friends and fellow growers that would get together several times a month, and party and trade our products. And, after the close call, we would not tell any outsiders where we were to meet or where we were to party. And this meant nobody outside of the circle.

Over the years, the people in this group have stuck together. Some have families, some have passed away, and some just quit doing anything. You know, that when we were growing up on Tusquittee, you would hear very often that the people of Tusquittee were very clannish, and it is still so today.

Although there are a lot of outsiders moved into the community, they don't have a clue to what clannish means. Me, I am proud to be from this place called Tusquittee, and hope to live out my life here, although it has changed so very much.

When growing up, we could fish where we pleased and we could hunt where we pleased. Now it is all posted property. Everywhere you look, people have put up posted signs, and if this is not enough, they have to have a road named after them, or a mountain, or the water falls, or a creek.

Well, this is fine and good because I have something that most folks will never have: I HAVE ENOUGH; THE CIRCLE IS UNBROKEN.

When We Were Kids

Growing up on Cold Branch, we had our chores to do every day. We were up at 5:00 every morning, we had breakfast, and then our chores began. We took turns milking the cows, feeding the hogs and the chickens. In the summer, when school was out, we would get our chores done as fast as we could, then it was play time.

We would hunt for spring lizards up the many river branches. We would also look for ginseng, which we would sell in early fall. On some of our trips to the woods, we would happen across a still site where we would stop and play the day away. Everyone who made whiskey did so mostly at night.

I can remember sitting in the living room at home, looking out the front window and seeing the neighbors walk in front of the fire under the still; they were on every spring branch around here. We were taught not to say anything about anyone or what they did. It was the code of the mountains.

In the summer, we had to keep the farm up. We had to hoe corn and tobacco and the vegetable garden. When fall came, we got to stay out of school a few days to help cut the tobacco, and then to work it into bands where it was ready for market. This farming would come in handy in the future, for me anyway.

Sometimes we got to go to town, but not very often. We would go to Murphy once a year. My dad would buy one bottle of soda pop and the four of us kids had to share. Oh boy, look out if one thought the other took too big a swallow! I believe I was 14 before I had a soda pop by myself.

All the roads were gravel or worse. We had local grocery stores: Arb Martin's down at the forks of the road, or C.J. Ellers over the mountain. We had no TV. We had electric installed in 1951, but we only had electric lights for many years. We had a spring in the front yard, and one of our chores was to carry in water for cooking and bathing. For a bathroom we had an outhouse. Most everyone had one. We had a two-seater with a burlap sack hung over the door.

A big year for us was 1955. We put a pump in the spring and lights in the house. A year later, we got the first TV on Cold Branch. After that we had lots of company every Saturday night; they came to watch the Grand Old Opry. Mom didn't allow them all to smoke or curse in the house, so at intermission they all hit the door to go outside.

We had an incredible life. It was very simple. We all got a new pair of shoes for Christmas, but we would only wear them when we had to. All summer we would go bare foot. Our feet would get so tough we would stomp chestnuts out of their husks. At Christmas time, we would each get one toy, usually it was homemade.

But we learned how to make something out of not too much. At a young age, I took the motor off my dad's garden tiller and put it on my bicycle to make a motor bike. Boy, did I get a whupping for that! I had to put it back, but not before I got my share of riding. I guess that was what started my interest in motor biking, which I did a lot of when I got older.

We went to Elf Schoolhouse for our first eight years. At Elf School, they was eight grades and only four teachers. I remember one time my teacher told us to write a story and use our 'magination, so I wrote a story about how we would one day fly planes just like we drive cars now, and we would have streets and stop signs in the sky. I guess she liked it, because I got an A+ for that one. I believe I still got that 'magination—I ain't worn it out yet!

When I was in the grade number eight, our principal Maurice Kitchens came into the classroom and asked for all the students who hadn't ever used a telephone to stand up. Two thirds of the class stood up. Well, he lined us up in his office and let every one of us call his secretary, Ruby Patterson, whom he had sent to her house behind the school. He let each one of us call her. Then he explained why: he said he didn't want us going into high school not ever having used a phone.

Young Howard

Me and Tony

Me and Tony, we grew up together back in the "70s. We water-skied with my brother Charlie every weekend and almost every afternoon after work. Charlie and I had went together and bought an old boat from Dan McGlamary. We ran that old thing until it wore plum out, then we went and bought a new engine and ran it for years.

Well, me and old Tony, we bought us one of them mountain bikes. Almost every weekend we would go to the mountains and ride. One Friday we got together about noon time and decided to go to Nantahala River. We decided to meet at 4:00 and leave from my house. When he showed up, he had a friend with him from Atlanta. This feller's name was Kenny Hall. I had never seen him before.

Well, we loaded our stuff on the bikes and away we went. It was pretty cold although it was January right around the 1st. We asked Kenny iffin he had plenty of clothes; he said he was covered. When we got to Tyler Creek on Nantahala River, it was already dark. A couple of years before, a bunch of us guys had got together and built a pretty nice camping shed. This place, it was right on the river, so we set our fishing poles and built a fire.

We started unpacking our packs and sleeping bags. Tony and me, we had been camping all along and were pretty well prepared. I knew when Kenny pulled out that Wal-Mart sleeping bag that he was in real trouble. That thing, it wasn't more than a quilt with a zipper.

Well, Tony and me, we pulled out the antifreeze: we both had a jug of liquor and a big bag of smoke—the left handed kind that we grew ourselves. We fixed something to eat and had a good fire going in the stove. It wasn't too bad cold as long as we stayed close to the stove. Well, about 10:00 it started getting real cold; the temperature was a little below zero. We decided to hit the sack.

My sleeping bag, it was made of duck down and Tony's, it was down-filled too. I went right to sleep and after a while I thought I heard something rattling. Well, what I heard was Kenny's teeth chattering. I woke Tony up and said "I don't think he is going to make it".

That man was real close to freezing.

Well, I have this goose down coat I always carry with me camping in the winter. This coat has six pounds of down in it. I handed it to poor old Kenny and was he ever glad to see that coat! I do believe that coat saved his life that night. The next morning when we got up, I think Kenny had had about enough of the river. It was now about ten degrees below zero.

When we had eaten breakfast, we packed up our gear and tried to get the bikes started. Tony and I had Honda four-stroke bikes, and they started, finally. Well, Kenny, he had one of them Yamahas. That thing was frozen and would not even turn over. We pushed it in the camp, right up against the stove, built up the fire real big, and about an hour later it broke loose. We finally got it started, and back to Hayesville we came. I believe that broke Kenny from ever going camping with us again.

Well, time, it moved on and we kept on riding every chance we got. About every time we went riding we would end up crashing out. On Sundays we would meet up at "the cut" we called it: me, Tony, Dudley, Rob, Rick, Rod, Jimmy, and Curtis most of the time. They was about 15 or 20 of us, and we would take off and ride to the spring on Clear Creek. There we stopped and had a shot of courage and a smoke, then off we would go.

One Sunday, we all got started and lined out headed for the Tusquitee Bald. We were about to where Clear Creek crosses the road. I was behind the others and feeling my oats. Well, there were two rows of bikes, and I took off down the middle of them. Just as they were about to cross the creek, I caught up with the front. I hit the creek about one bike length in front of the two front bikes. When they got there, well, you can imagine—soaked! I was the target for a long time after that.

We all headed for Old Road Gap. Once there, we stopped for a shot of courage before heading up the trail to the Choga Lookoff. The Big Choga Lookoff is a cliff of rock about 500 feet high and straight off. Once, a man was riding his horse up through there, and he got off to lead him by the Lookoff. As he was about to pass it, the horse started acting up. The guy started pulling on the bridle and the horse backed off of the cliff. About all that was left was the saddle.

We went from there to the Signal Bald which is pretty high, but you still look up to see the Tusquitee Bald. Once on top of the Tusquitee Bald, you can see all the way into Georgia and Tennessee. We went from there down to the Bald Springs, where we stopped for a nooning. We had a drink of the best water that there is in the state.

From there we went to the Pot Rock Bald. This Bald was named by the Indians because there is a rock there that has a bowl carved in the top. That is where the Indians made medicine. From there we went to the Johnson Bald; it is pretty high there too. And from there we went down the rim trail to Carver's Gap and came off on the Fires Creek Road.

The next Sunday we were riding again. This time we were stopped at the Compass Hole. Tony, he was doing wheelies on his bike when it ran right out from under him. He was doing pushups at 30 miles per hour. His hands, chin, and knees were skinned pretty bad. We picked him up, carried him down to the creek and washed the blood off. He took off his socks and wrapped his hands and away we went up Tusquittee.

I was in the front when we got to Perry Mill Creek. There was a foot log to cross about 30 foot long, or, you could ford the creek. The ford was too easy so across I went. We had done this many times. I never thought to look back until quite a ways up the creek, and when I did, I didn't see Tony. Well, I turned around and went back down the road. When I got there I couldn't find Tony.

About that time Ralph Plott drove up. I ask him where Tony went. He says that he was in front of him when they left Compass. About that time, I think I see something in the creek. It was Tony's bike; he had missed the foot log and into Tusquittee Creek he had went. We all got together and fished out his bike. Then he looked at me and said enough is enough; he would not get back on that bike.

Well, we talked Ralph into riding it back to his house. I don't think he ever got back on that bike again. I couldn't blame him; that thing had whopped him pretty good that day. I think that day taught us all a lesson. We all quit riding bikes and started riding in cars. It wasn't long before Tony was married to Vickie. She was a lot safer than any bike. I guess we all had to grow up sooner or later and settle down!

Tuck and Mettie

Tuck Dowell, he was a quiet man and made a little moonshine now and again. One time, he was in the woods making a little shine and had been doing it for a while, when he thought he heard something making a noise in the leaves.

Tuck, he was always a little spooked by nature and was this day ready for anything. All of a sudden, a revenuer stepped out of the woods. Tuck, well, he took off to running, and when he ran he went straight up the mountain. These government men were in pretty good shape but not compared to what Tuck was.

Well, up the mountain Tuck ran. The man chasing him knew right away that he wasn't going to catch Tuck, so he yelled "Stop or I will shoot."

Well, Tuck, he stopped and turned around and yelled "Ye ain't got no right to shoot. Ye ain't!"

And away Tuck went. They didn't see Tuck again for a long time and they didn't catch him, neither. As most people know, the law has to be within 20 feet, or, if it's dark, they have to touch you. Tuck, he eased by that one with luck on his side.

Well, another time, Tuck, he was pretty sharp when it came to work. One day he was plowing his corn field when a man came to get a jug of moonshine.

Tuck said "I need to get my corn plowed out today".

The man, he said that if Tuck would go get him some moonshine that he would plow for him.

Tuck thought a minute and said "Well, if you need it that bad I'll go and get it fer ya, but it will take a purty good while."

The man said that was ok with him, and Tuck gave him the reins of the horse and left.

First he went down through the field and into the woods. What the man didn't know was that Tuck slipped back to the house, where he sat down for a rest which lasted until he figured the man was about finished plowing the field. Then Tuck, he got up and went out of the house where he reached under the floor and got the jug of moonshine. He went back into the woods and circled around to the field. When he came back into the field it was by the same route he had left. Tuck, he had suckered that man pretty good, and the man never knew better, but he got his liquor and that's all that mattered.

A few years later, Mettie his wife, she got pregnant, and all the men around, they liked to tease Tuck about what it would be: a boy or a girl. Story has it, when Mettie's time was up and the baby was due, all the men got together with Doc Staton. When it came, they told Tuck that it was a girl.

Now, Tuck, he was disappointed and would have nothing to do with the baby. He said that Mettie could take care of it. The neighbors, they forgot all about what they had said about it being a girl, when in fact it was a boy. When the baby was about four or five, Mettie, she got sick and was laid up. This left Tuck to care for the child.

Saturday night came, and, as everyone knows, that was bath night. Well, Tuck, he was going to bathe the child. When he took its clothes off, Mettie heard him holler. He said "Lord God Mettie, it's a man child!"

Tuck, he got him a job with the state. Now, everyone knows how hard the state crews work. One day he was watching a man on a machine when a dog walked right up and pissed on his leg. Well, Tuck, he just looked down and said to the dog "Iffin I had another shovel I would kill you."

That meant he was not going to get off of the one he was leaning on.

Well, Tuck, he would always leave the house at the same time every morning. He lived across Tusquittee Creek and had to cross on a bridge. When you got to the road it was pretty steep up into it. Well, one day when Tuck was coming out of his driveway, he ran right into Smiley Mull.

Now Smiley, he had him a nice 1954 Ford car. Tuck, he plowed right into the side of it. They both got out of the car and Tuck said "Smiley, you should have knowed I would be coming out of my driveway about now!"

They didn't call the law or anything and I don't remember who paid for what, but they settled it amongst themselves.

Tuck's son Louis, he was a real go-getter when the mail came. He would go and get it and that was about all you would get out of him. Tuck, he bought Louis a mini bike. Now, Louis, he's about 6'4" tall and them knees, they would stick well above the handlebars. It was quite a sight to see him ride that thing, but ride it he did.

After Tuck retired, him and Mettie, they both got real sick and were put into the nursing home down to town. Louis, he stayed on the creek for a long time until they both passed away, then came to find out that he owed the county a lot of money for their health care. The county, they took the property from Louis and sold it. Louis was supposed to get an acre and a trailer house and get to live on the place.

Well, it didn't work out that way. I don't know all the details but Louis lives on Shooting Creek now in a trailer house. Every day you will see him come across Cold Branch headed for the old homestead, where he goes and sits for hours.

It just weren't right what the county did to him but I guess it is what it is. Sorry, Louis. You sure got screwed out of everything.

Uncle Wade Ledford

Uncle Wade was married to my grandmother's oldest daughter Robilee. They had three kids: Kenneth was the oldest, then Betty Jean, and then Charles. Well, Uncle Wade, he made a little moonshine from time to time.

He and a friend had a still set up on the head of Scataway. That is above Hiawassee, GA, toward Clayton. Someone stole Uncle Wades' still and he thought it was old man Steve Rowland. He thought so because he saw Steve's old horse going over the ridge with it tied to its back. What he didn't know was that Steve had loaned his horse to someone else; they were the ones that stole the still.

Wade, he came back to find it gone. He and his partner, they got out the old sawed off 12 gauge shotgun. They then headed for Tusquittee to find Steve. As they crossed Cold Branch, they came to Steve's house to find him gone. They asked his wife Zadie where he was. She said she didn't know. Well, Wade, he said he would come back later and settle things with Steve, then he and his buddy went on down to the next house where Lassie Parker lived.

They were several people there at Lassie's house and some were drinking, and some weren't. Well, Wade, he was feeling his oats, as they say, and accused Clifton of getting his still and said he would shoot him.

Well, Cliff took it as a threat, so he pulled out his .38 special and shot him in the head. He was dead before he hit the kitchen floor. The Lathum boy that was with Wade, ran out the front door and got about halfway to the road before Cliff shot him in the legs. He made it a little ways down the road before he fell. Well, about that time Wade's wife Robilee was coming up the road, so they picked up what was left of Wade's brains in a rag and threw them in the branch.

This was how it was told by Grandma Stamey: she said they heard the gun fire, and she told her mother someone was shooting down at Lassie's house. While they were waiting for the law to come, they pulled the boards up on the kitchen floor and turned them over so they could not see the blood. They told the law that the killing had taken place out in front of the house. The law questioned Cliff about it. He told them it was self defense and they let him go.

After the funeral, my Aunt Robilee, she loaded up her kids and went to Cleveland, Tennessee to the Church of God Orphanage. There she worked and cooked and cleaned and raised her three kids in more tame surroundings than Tusquittee. Later she moved to Kannapolis, N.C. where she worked in the Church of God orphanage for many more years until she retired. Then she came back to Tusquittee and helped take care of her mother until she passed away on October 12, 1978.

The Lathum boy, he survived the shooting and moved away. Cliff, he married Maudine and moved to the Stamey Cove where he lived out his life, and for a hobby—wouldn't you just know it—he made miniature stills and sold them all over the U.S. Well, as for Aunt Robilee's kids, the oldest, Kenneth, became a school teacher and held two P.H.D's in education. He taught for 35 years in Ohio. Betty Jean, she married a preacher and lived in South Carolina. The youngest son Charles, he worked for the veteran's hospital in Asheville, N.C. He passed away several years ago.

Kenneth, he is still kicking pretty high at the young age of 85. He and I attended a birthday party for Cecil Parker a short time ago in Cleveland, Tennessee.

Aunt Robilee, she never remarried.

Tusquittee Moonshine

Tusquittee, having all that good water and the great depression going on, people had to make it the best they could. So about everyone started making corn whiskey. They were no factories and they was no work so folks turned to something they were good at doing.

It was not long before it went nationwide; people from all over the country wanted Tusquittee moonshine. My dad and nine or ten of his friends got together and thought they would try and make a little money, being it was so scarce. So they had old man Jim Young make them two stills at 500 gallons each. Now, old Jim could not read or write even enough to spell his own name, but he could build a still within a quart of what you might want, by sight alone.

Well, they got their stills and set them up about one half mile up Matlock Creek. They started making and were putting out 1000 gallons weekly. They hired two of Ever Cowart's flatbed trucks and she hired the Lathum boys to drive them for her. Once a week they hauled a load of shine to the railroad depot in Asheville, NC.

Well, back then they was only the old road which went right through the middle of Franklin. Of course, the boys hauled only at night, so as they were going through town—one following the other—a red light caught them, so they had to stop.

While they were waiting for it to change, a town cop came over the hill, his lights shining into the back of the truck. They didn't even have it covered up! Well, that, needless to say, didn't go over too good with the cops.

Well, them two boys jumped out of them trucks and ran like the devil himself was after them. The two made their way back to Hayesville. Upon their arrival, they promptly contacted Ms. Cowart to tell what had happened. She then reported her trucks stolen.

These two loads of illegal moonshine attracted the attention of the A.T.F., or as we called them back then the revenuers. They started to look for the source, but came up empty.

Meanwhile, my dad got his call to the military. He was inducted into the Army, thus sent to Fort Bragg, NC. Meanwhile, the other guys kept on making liquor on Matlock Creek. The revenuers sent in an informant undercover. One of the guys making moonshine started to drink while in town one night and bragged about the operation to this informant.

The undercover guy, he said he would like to buy a large amount of moonshine. The next day, this good old boy, he showed up at the still site with this man. They were caught and didn't even know it.

Meanwhile, they had hired our neighbor to cut and drag in wood for cooking mash. He worked 40 hours a week, and was paid for himself and his team of horses. The undercover guy kept coming back buying more whiskey. He was also taking pictures for evidence.

Meanwhile, my dad was shipped to the Pacific to fight the Japanese. A little later in the month, here come the revenuers. At the time of the bust, the guys had saved $90,000 in cash; they had it stuffed in a pillow case.

They were handcuffed and taken to jail, then were sent on to federal prison for four years. They never recalled my dad for trial; they said he had enough problems and was getting punished enough by the War.

Howard as Moonshiner

Moonshine Still

Milus and Delia Woods

Milus and Delia were an odd couple. They both were into making moonshine for most of their lives. Now, Milus, he had him a still up on Perry Creek but he would not tell Delia where it was, and Delia, she had her one hid in the thicket behind the house.

Well now, that Delia, she was a little smarter than Milus when it came to hiding a still. Delia, she took her a piece of pipe and buried it under the ground where it could not be found; that way the law could not find it that easy. Well, I guess that Delia's moon was a little better than Milus' was. I guess he would put up an argument, but the taste told it all.

Well, they were as close as a couple could get except when it come down to business. Once a year, the Georgia Mountain Fair would come to Hiawassee, Georgia and that was their favorite time of the year. They went every night that it was in town. Delia, she was pretty good at playing a banger. She would get up on that stage and plat her heart out every night, and Milus, he would egg it on. This would go on for a good two weeks.

The Georgia Mountain Fair is still going on today. The big difference is that they did away with a lot of the attractions, such as the wildlife and the reptiles. I remember when I was working over in the birch cove, we were logging and we would see snakes every day in the summer. One summer, we caught a big rattlesnake and I put it in my lunch box. It was crawling across my brother Charlie's foot. Well, we caught that thing and we took it to the fair and gave it to them. The fair also had all kinds of wildlife. It was located in the middle of Hiawassee where the old school was.

Milus and Delia, they raised her grandson Ralph Plott. Now, you talk about a wild one; he was as wild as a buck deer. Ralph, he was about a year older than I was and we were best friends for years and years. We would haul Milus' and Delia's moonshine to the buyer. For payment, Delia would pay to keep Ralph's cars running faster than the law, and they sure was.

When Ralph graduated from school he moved to Atlanta. There he went to work for his dad and made a fine electrician. But every weekend he would come home to Tusquittee.

A few years later, Milus, he died and Delia, she was so lonely. She had no way to go anywhere, so I would go up and take her wherever she needed to go. Sometimes on the weekends we would go up there and play cards and drink beer and moonshine, and maybe enjoy a joint or two. The years, they went by and Ralph, he came home less and less. When spring would come and the ramps started to come up, on Sunday mornings Delia would call me and say "I have the corn bread and taters ready. Let's go to the ramp patch and cook dinner."

I couldn't say no so I would go and pick her up and we would get down the road. She would say "Let us stop and get Pain Mull and take her with us."

So we did. When we got to the ramp patch—which was over yonder in the deep gap on the head of Buck Creek—they would set up the camp and I would go to the woods and dig the ramps. Meanwhile, they were cooking the taters and frying the native trout.

Now, you talk about good vittles, that was some of the best. We would do this about every Sunday until the ramps were too big to cook. Then we would go and dig a batch of them, and Delia and Pain would pickle and can them. After they had canned all they wanted, we would get some and put them in the freezer. A few years later when the dehydrator came out, I would go to the ramp patch and get me some, then when I got home I would cut them into pieces and put them in and dry them. After they dried, I would put them into a blender and make powder out of them. The powder could season most anything you hankered to.

A few years later, Pain and Delia were both passed on, but they left behind some of the best memories and these are more precious than money. I guess the only thing we leave behind us is what we give away.

Milus & Delia Woods House

Granny Alice Cothren and Sons

Granny Alice was a nice old lady. She was old the first time I laid eyes on her. She and her son Gene, they came to my Dad's house and asked to rent the old house he had bought form Vierce Roland. Well, that old house was built back in 1936 and was built out of one big tree. This tree came from the forks of Perry Mill Creek and Tusquittee. The tree was so large that it took a double bladed saw mill to saw it.

It so happened that Floyd Saltz had a mill like that close to where the tree was. They had Floyd work the tree up for them, loaded the lumber on wagons and hauled it to Cold Branch. Vierce, he lived there for a long time. When he told my Dad it was for sale and he wanted the big price of $400 dollars, well Dad, he bought it, did a little remodeling and rented it to Granny Alice for $20 a month. She lived there for ten years and then raised her own rent to $35 a month.

About every other day she would holler for one of us boys to come and fix the water. It was brought by gravity and would stop up real often with silt. The water tank, it was about a quarter of a mile up the mountain above a rock cliff. Well, my dad sent me that day. I got to the water tank, cleaned it out and started back down the hill. That whole place up there was covered with kudzu vines. When about halfway down, I stepped on a copperhead snake.

Well, I commenced to run. I ran a little ways, stopped, looked down and that snake, it was still there! I took to running again. I ran right past Granny's house, I ran right past Grandma Stamey's, and that copperhead was still there. I ran right over the hill toward home and the harder I ran the faster the snake was.

When I got home, that thing was still there. I was hollering real loud. My brother, he came out and looked, then stomped that copperhead to death. Come to find out it had bit the heel of my shoe and got hung with its fangs; that was the reason I could not out run it.

About every day or so, Gene, he would come down and want to go to the store down at the forks. Well, it turned out that Arb Martin had helped find Gene a girlfriend. Her name was Fanny and she was from Tiger, GA. They dated a while, then decided to get married. Fanny, she was a good woman for Gene.

Now, Gene, he never learned to tell the truth; lying came natural for him. People said that the truth was in him, but it never did come out. One day he came down to our house.

He said "Son, I need for you and Charlie and Edward to be pallbearers".

We said "What's wrong, Gene? Did someone die?"

He said "No, but Fanny, she is real sick and I didn't want to wait too long to get you guys to help. I think she is going to die".

Well, Fanny, she didn't die that time, but later on she did.

Gene, he would come every day. One of us would drive him to the store, and Arb, he would bring him home. Sometimes, Gene would come down to Dad's and take us boys coon and possum hunting. Now Gene, he was afraid of the dark. Us boys, we would turn the lantern off and he would freak out.

He would say "Son, light that lantern, you are making the others skeered".

It wasn't long and Gene, he was married again. This time he married Gladys Maney. Now, Gladys, she was a good woman, just a little slow. She was the perfect mate for Gene.

My dad had a real good coon dog. Her name was June. One night Gene and Sam Stamey came down. Gene, he said "Joe, we want to borrow your coon dog."

Well, dad, he would let him use her. They went up Matlock Creek where the dog started trailing a coon, or at least they thought it was.

Well, the dog, it trees up on the top of the ridge under a rock cliff. Sam and Gene, they get to the top, and Gene, says" it's Old Dad, it's Old Dad". Well, Sam, he isn't sure that it really is a coon and says so. Gene, he won't hear of it, so he gathers up a little fire wood and he puts it in the hole under the rock cliff. He lights the wood.

Gene, he steps back and says to Sam "It's Old Dad; he will come out in a real quick".

Well, Old Dad, he didn't come right out, so Gene pulls the fire back, gets on his hands and knees and starts to go in the hole. The dog, she sees what is going on and runs past Gene.

Well, the dog grabbed Old Dad, only it wasn't a coon. It so happened to be a bob cat and a very pissed off one. Out of the hole came Gene, the cat was a hold of his head and the dog was a hold of the cat.

Down over the mountain they went. As they rolled past Sam, Gene, he yells "Get it off, it's a panther, it's a panther!"

Well, Sam, he couldn't do anything for laughing, and they rolled all the way to the bottom. Finally, the cat decided to turn Gene loose. He was a little skinned up and a whole lot scared. It was a long time before Gene borrowed the dog again.

Granny Cothren, she had another son. His name was Thirl. He lived up the road a little ways in the gap. He and his wife Ethel, they had twelve kids: ten of them survived, and nine of them moved to Washington State. Every summer some of them would come back home on vacation.

Well, the kids, they would get out and loafer. They were coming home later and later every night. Loman, their dad, would ask "Where have you kids been?"

They would say "Watching X rated movies."

Loman, he couldn't figure out where they were going, so one night he followed them.

Granny, she never had curtains on her windows. He followed the kids to Granny's driveway. When he got there he looked in her yard. Sure enough, there was the group of kids sitting outside of Gene and Gladys's window. They were in a circle. Into the bedroom came Gene and Gladys. They stripped off their clothes and started having SEX. That was all it took for Loman; he started rounding up kids and sending them home, the mystery solved.

The next summer, Thirl's boys invited Gene and Gladys to come visit them in Washington. That fall, Gene, he came down and asked my uncle O.A. Blankenship for a ride to the bus station in Murphy. My uncle dropped them off after helping them purchase their tickets. He then came back home and called Thirl's boys in Washington warning them of Gene's and Gladys' trip.

Upon arriving in Longview, Washington, neither one had ever used a telephone, so they didn't know to make a call. Well, Thirl's boys had been checking periodically to see when they would get there. They never dreamed it would take three weeks to make that trip. They had given up on old Gene and Gladys.

Gene, he hired a feller outside the bus station to take them to Cathlamet. That was the town where most of the boys lived. Upon arriving there, they went first to Kenny Cothren's house. When Kenny came to the door, he could tell they had not taken a shower since leaving North Carolina. He asked Gene if he would like a shower. Gene said no, they had taken one before they had left home.

Well, Kenny, he said "Let's go down to Loman's house."

Meanwhile, Kenny's wife called ahead and told Loman the situation. He met them at the door with a bar of soap and a towel, and insisted on them taking a bath.

Well, they rested a few days, then one afternoon when the boys came in from work Gene was not there. Gladys was sitting on the porch. They asked where Gene was and she said that he went to town to the bar.

When Gene first got to town, he had gone into the Columbia Saloon, ordered him a beer and sat down at a table. A guy stopped to talk to Gene, and he knew at once he weren't from around there. They talked for a little while, the guy telling Gene a story about hunting. Gene, he listened for a bit, and then it was his turn. Well, he started telling about a panther he had seen, and it started to get good. The more Gene talked, the more he would add to his lie.

Well, the people, they started to gather around their table. The more people that gathered around, the bigger the lie got. After a little while it was getting obvious that Gene was not just stretching the truth, but telling one of the biggest lies he could make up. About the time that the other guys were about to figure it out, Loman came in. Well, Gene, he was about to climax with the story when one of the people listening asked "Just how big was this panther, Mr. Cothren?"

Gene, he said it was about ten feet wide and six feet long and weighed fifteen pounds. Of course it didn't make sense! It looked like you had jumped a covey of quail as the people scattered, as they saw he was so full of it! Loman, he gathered up Gene and headed home.

The next day was the opening of elk season. Of course the next morning, Gene, he wanted to go. They asked him what gun he would like to use. He said a 20 gauge shotgun with buckshot. They all laughed. They found Gene a gun and away they went.

Upon arriving in the woods, they all got together and decided to put Gene up on an old growth stump. For the ones who have never seen one, it's a huge tree that had swelled out and had to be cut down about twenty feet off the ground.

Gene, he crawled up on that stump and sat down. The others, they went on with their hunting. They hunted all day and saw nothing. When they went back to pick up Gene, he was waiting at the road. When they stopped and asked him did he see anything, he says "I killed Old Dad."

Well they knew him and didn't believe him and told him to get in the truck. He would not get in, and insisted that he had killed an elk.

Loman, he finally gave in to him and said "All right show me Old Dad."

Well, Gene, he started down over the hill. When they got to where they had left him, there at the bottom of the stump laid a big bull elk. It seems Gene didn't lie that time. He had skunked all of them.

A few days later they left Washington again on a bus. You know the people on the bus were entertained all the way home.

Well, Christmas rolled around and on Tusquittee that meant it was time for a party. Granny Cothren, she always had a party at her house. That meant the word got out and about everyone around would come.

She sent word up the creek to Eb Mull's house. Now, Eb, he had a passel of kids and just about all of them could play some sort of musical instrument. Eb, he played the fiddle; Ruby, she played the guitar; Kenneth, he played the mandolin, and Gordon, he played anything. They all got together that night at Granny Alice's house. They had a little wine and a little homebrew -that's homemade beer- and of course, there was the moonshine.

The party was really getting hot around 10:00 and people were getting real loose. Forrest Moore, he was really on one. They were all dancing and having a good time and nobody had seen Forrest for a while. Well, May Mull, she went outside to look. She hollered for him and he answered and told her to get help, he had fallen into a hole. May, she went inside and told Gene. He went out to look and he found him.

Well, Gene, he came down to our house and knocked on the door. My dad went to the door and opened it.

Gene said "Joe you got to come quick. Forrest, he has fell in the well".

Dad, he got me out of bed, and we went up there expecting the worst. We pulled in, got out of the truck and walked up to the house.

Here come Gene. We followed him and above the house, there was Forrest. He was standing in the septic tank and crap was up to his armpits.

Oh my, what a smell! We finally pulled him out of there, got the water hose and started washing him off. The temperature was about 10 degrees. Well, by the time we had him washed off he was about iced over, and so were we. Another great year on Tusquittee; everyone survived.

Maynard and the Sheriff

Maynard and the Sheriff were colorful characters. This is their story.

They both were born on Tusquittee and were about the same age. What they also had about the same was getting drunk. Well, the Sheriff, he never harmed anyone or anything except himself. He and Maynard would drink most anything that had alcohol in it.

One time they got drunk and decided to go to Alaska. The Sheriff had a 1960 Ford station wagon he bought cheap after the Clay County sheriff was done with it. They loaded the old car up with just about everything they owned, and left for Alaska. No one is quite sure how long it took to get there but they made it.

I guess Sheriff found a job after arriving there. He wasn't a lazy man; he just didn't like real hard work. It didn't matter to Maynard what the job was as he would go along with anything. They lived in a camp ground. Now, Maynard, he could cook just about anything they was to cook. You could call him a gourmet in country cooking.

The boys, they stayed in Alaska most of the summer. Finally old Neil—that is what they named the old station wagon, it was after its previous owner Sheriff Neil Kitchens—Old Neil, he laid down on them. So they had no car and were over 6000 miles from home.

Sheriff, he went to the junk yard to see what they would offer for the car. The guy came over and looked at it and said "You will have to pay me to take it off your hands."

Maynard and Sheriff, they packed up what they could carry and headed south down the Alcan Highway. About ten days later, they made it to the U.S. border. There they were stuck for several days. Maynard said it was so cold, that the air mattress they slept on froze to the ground.

Finally they made it to Cathlamet, Washington where my older brother lives. There they stayed a couple of weeks and found a job hauling hay for an old farmer named Roy Jaspers. Well, Roy's daughter-in-law was from Japan. She knew how to make tomato wine. The boys were in hog heaven again.

A few days later they hit the road again toward California. They made it to Needles where they found work picking grapes in a vineyard. They ate more grapes than they put in the baskets! They made $40 between them. Maynard, he asked Sheriff what they should do with the money, buy food or something? Sheriff, he just looked at Maynard and said "That is a stupid question."

They bought alcohol.

On the road again, they flagged down a hippie in a Volkswagen van. For three or four days they traveled. The hippie, he asked them the shortest route to Florida. Of course the route went through Hayesville, NC.

Once in Hayesville they looked for a ride home which was only five or six miles away. They ended up walking all the way home. It was as far as they had to walk the whole trip.

After a few days' rest, it was on the road again for Sheriff. He found a job driving a truck. Maynard, he went to work for the telephone company. This went on for several years.

On the weekend, they would get together and drink beer, maybe a little moonshine. Well, one Saturday night after consuming many cases of beer, Maynard, he looked over at the Sheriff and said "You know, I would like to wake up in the mornin' with palm trees over my head and sand between my toes."

Well, he had no idea what he started. When Maynard awoke the next morning, they were in Key West, Florida, the car parked as far as it would go out in the ocean, with everyone passed out drunk. He learned right then you don't say anything about going anywhere when the sheriff was drinking.

They got back home and went back to work. They worked for a while, then one weekend Sheriff came driving a new Dodge Charger home. It was lime green. The first place they went was the beer store on Bell Creek. When they pulled in, Sheriff opened the trunk, stripped out the carpet, poured in five bags of ice, and here come Maynard with the beer. They filled the trunk with ten cases, then covered it with ice. Back to the Compass Hole they came and started to drink.

A neighbor had seen the car parked there for a couple of days, when he told his wife he should check on them and see if they were still alive. That was a mistake. When he got there, they got him in the car and it was the first time in years he had been drunk. His wife was worried about him, and upon checking, she proceeded to take him home. He never checked on them anymore as his wife would not allow it.

The boys, they survived that one and the adventures continued.

Ray and Mattie

Ray and Mattie were what you would call the couple that was born to be together. Where you would see Ray, Mattie was not far away. They were married at a young age and were never apart for very long. They built their house where the old schoolhouse sat at one time. As a matter of fact, it was the one that all of the kids back then attended. And it was the place that the First Church of God people had their first meetings. Ray's father, Harrison, owned a large tract of property where the offspring of his sons and daughters now live.

Well, they had two girls, and one son named Stanley. Stanley was always one who liked to make a little moonshine, and would sell a little, and maybe even on occasion take a little swig. One time he was making a little liquor up on the mountain above his house. Back then they made it at night so the law could not see the smoke from their fire. Well, Ray, he had been working all night and was just finishing up at the break of day, when he heard someone walking down the old logging road up on the ridge.

Now Ray, he was pretty smart about making moonshine. When he set his still up for running, he didn't put it on the branch like most people would; instead he run him a pipe for the water over the ridge and down a dry holler. Well, when the law came looking for his still, they would always look on a branch. The reason for this was because a man has to have water to make moonshine. The water is for the condenser, or worm, as most folks call it.

Now, to make moonshine, you would start with 50 gallons of water in an oak barrel, then take 50 pounds of corn ground up pretty fine, then put 25 pounds in the water, and then you add 50 pounds of sugar and stir it up real good. Then you put in it a gallon of malt corn ground up pretty fine. You then let it set until it quits working off, (you can tell this by when it quits rolling or bubbling. If you try to run it off too soon the moon will look milky, so it is important to let it finish working.) You then pour it into a copper still and fire it up.

You have to be careful not to get it too hot because it will scorch your mash and the liquor will be firey. Now, this 50 gallons will make about six or seven gallons; it depends on how cold your water is.

Well anyway, Ray heard them coming and stayed real quiet. When they got by where he was hiding, he followed them down the ridge, staying just out of sight. When they got to the road, he was already in the house, safe.

Now, Ray and Mattie, they started out young and in love, and it has only grown to be stronger and stronger as the years have gone by. Still today, when you see them out, they are together. Every now and then, I try to get up there to visit them and see how they are doing, and always the subject he loves to talk about is making moonshine.

I guess the last time I was up there, we got to talking about making a little run, and Mattie, she said "Now Ray, you know you all had better not be a doin' that."

Ray, he will say a little drink never hurt anyone. Then Mattie, she will just look at us and smile, and you can just see the love she still has for the old fellow. All couples should have such love. He is in his late 80s and still has a sharp mind and still a little spunk left. They still live in the same house and still on the family farm. You don't find many people that happy.

The Tusquittee Church of God

The Tusquittee Church of God was founded in 1910. Reverend John Davis was the pastor. But after doing a little research in reality, the first revival was held at the Tusquittee school house. This school was located about a quarter of a mile above the mouth of Chairmaker Branch.

It sat on property owned by Ray Stillwell; as a matter of fact he still lives there. Ray's mother Ellie Stillwell asked Ray if she could have a revival in the old school building. Of course he said it was ok. She contacted Reverend Emerson Davenport to come preach. According to Ray, the revival lasted several days. After the revival was over, Ellie and a few more people got together and contacted Reverend Davis.

Well, the church was built and used for a while, then one night it was set afire and burned. From what I could find out it was Glen Martin and Eagle Morgan who did the burning.

The people were not discouraged. Again the church was built, this time in a different spot to the forks in the road where the church stands today. It was used for a while; then it burned again. This time it was Glen Martin and Clem Passmore. They had been drinking and turned mean.

Well, the people built it back again in the same spot where it stands today. My dad, his brothers, and a lot of other folks got together and did the work. They were many preachers that preached there. The one that really impressed me was a man from Cleveland, Tennessee. His name was Robert Orr. He and his wife Jo, they would drive all the way from Cleveland every weekend. That was a drive of about 90 miles one way. They had five girls and they were all baby dolls, from the youngest to the oldest. Now, us boys, we thought the world of the preacher and found out that he was in the service and held the rank of sergeant, so we started calling him Sarge.

Well, the name, it stayed with him for many years and until his death a few weeks ago, I still thought of him as Sarge. Four of his girls, they favored him a whole lot but the youngest one, Yvonne, she had his red hair and blue eyes and big smile. After leaving the church they would come back to my dad's house for a visit; usually they would have lunch with us. I hope they will stay in touch.

The church, it was remodeled a few years ago and was made bigger. Last year was the 100 years since the church was founded. I guess it was the first Church of God founded in North Carolina. The preacher now is Curt Ledford, a good man—a man of GOD—and he practices what he preaches.

Uncle Bob Allison

Bob Allison was a self-sufficient man. He lived on the head of Big Tuni Creek along with his wife Lassie. Uncle Bob owned what is now the Bob Allison Campground. He, along with his wife, owned about 1000 acres along Tuni Creek. He was a farmer and trapper. He and Lassie, they had three children: Luther, Hannah and Sam.

Now, Bob, he was a bit tight with his money. He would walk to the store on Tusquittee and bring a few chickens and eggs. This wasn't a short walk by no means; I guess it was between 10 or 12 miles one way to the store. My Grandpa Will, he owned the store and said that Bob would trade the chickens for what they needed. This would be salt or maybe dried beans, although most of the time they grew their own.

They also grew their own tobacco, corn and wheat, so they needed very little store goods. My dad, he told me that Uncle Bob would not buy shells for his gun to hunt squirrels. Instead, he would knock them out of a tree with rocks. That would make him as good as any ball player around.

Back then, most folks, they had hogs running loose in the woods. They would mark their ears with a slice or two or they would cut a notch in their ear. Each family would have their particular slice or number of notches. Back then, they were plenty of chestnut trees which were our version of old growth trees. People also let their cattle loose in the woods to range.

Now, Luther, Uncle Bob's oldest, he helped on the farm until he came of age to marry. He married a lady named Ruby Killian. They then moved to the state of Washington to a town called Vader. There, he and Ruby, they had a passel of kids.

Hannah was one of them. She married a Jones from Tusquittee the first time, and lived here for a while. Later she was married about four more times. The last, it was to Alexander Mohamed from Clayton, Georgia. She died in 1994, September 16th. Al, he lived several more years, and he died on January 3, 2009.

Sammy, he was the youngest of the kids. He married Mary Jo Patterson. WW II started and Sam, he went to the Army. He and my dad were sent at the same time. Both were sent to Fort Bragg in North Carolina. After basic training, Dad went to the Pacific Theatre and Sammy, he went to Europe where he was killed in action. The VFW post in Hayesville is named after Sammy and the Bristol boy.

Well, Uncle Bob, he wouldn't spend any money that anyone knew about; he would bury it. After his death, they found a lard bucket full of money under the front steps of the house. Aunt Lassie, she didn't want to live up on Tuni by herself, so she sold the property to the Andrews lumber company. They logged the land and then they sold it to the Forest Service. They then made the place into a campground for the public. What a lot of people don't know about is the railroad that came across Tuni Gap and down Tuni Creek to Tusquittee. This was the original Peavine railway; the old grade is still there in part.

Aunt Lassie, she moved to town for a while, and then she moved to Cold Branch where she lived until she met Wilburn Ledford. They moved over to Burnt Schoolhouse Ridge, where they had children. They had two that I know of: Beulah May and Howard. Howard, he went to Washington State when he was about 20 and was killed in a logging accident. Beulah May, she lived a prosperous life here in Clay County.

I went to visit Uncle Bob's grave the other day, and it took a while to find it. Only a rock marks the spot where he is buried. Later, I am going back and place a tomb stone on his grave. I think he deserves one; he was truly a giant of a man. A lot of people camp in his shadow not even knowing who he truly was.

My Siblings

I have two brothers and a sister, and for the times it was considered a small family. The oldest of the kids is my sister Pat. She was always the smartest in book learning and went to college when she finished high school. She found a job in Hayesville and taught school there for over 30 plus years. During that time, she went on to classes and received her Master's degree, and lacks a few semesters having her doctorate in education. She now resides in Hayesville with her husband Sam and they have been married for many years.

Well now, my older brother Henry, he graduated high school in 1968 and left for the Washington State and never looked back. I guess he followed the Cothren boys and went to work where they and everyone who lives there works: in the woods logging, and fishing the Columbia River. Well, when he got settled, he sent for his girlfriend Glenda Shook and, upon arriving in state, they were married.

Well, Glenda, she had three kids from a previous marriage and they had two kids of their own. Well, times were pretty hard for them in a strange place and with all of those kids, but knowing Henry and Glen, they adjusted. She worked in a nursing home and he logged. The years, they went by and they did fairly well. Every year they would come back home for a couple of weeks, and in the later years the boys would come for the summer. They had four boys and one daughter.

A few years later their oldest boy was killed in a car accident. This was real hard for the both of them and the whole family. This incident started a whole new chapter in all of our lives. Henry and Glen, they went to school to learn how to take care of foster kids. I guess this was to help fill the void that was created from losing their son, Jody.

The years went by, and they came home less and less because they were busy raising kids. Well, they came one summer and to our surprise they had adopted another one; her name was Kelly and a she was a sweetheart. Henry said that at one time he had five kids in diapers, and they would line up on the floor every morning and say "I first, Papaw".

Meanwhile, I went to visit them for a couple of weeks and ended up staying for five years. While there, Henry and I and his wife built them a house. This house, it had fifteen rooms, with six bedrooms and four baths. This came in handy for fostering kids.

Henry's wife passed a few years ago, and we flew out for the services. When we were in the church, my sister-in-law Shirley asked the kids to stand up and be recognized. Only part of them could attend, and they were six pews full: about 35. A while back, I asked Henry how many kids they raised, and all he said was "a bunch". We then later counted up how many, and the number was 102!

I guess it takes a special kind of people to do what they did. Today, Henry has lots of grand kids and seven great grand kids. He will turn 62 in July. Henry now spends all of his time hunting and fishing in Alaska and several other states.

My younger brother Charlie, when we were growing up we never fought or had cross words. When he turned 20 he married Kathy Brendle and they were very happy. They had two girls: Alisha and Alice.

Charlie and I have worked together for 40 years, for the most part. That is, when I was not off loafering. Well, I guess old Charlie is about the best at figuring out the building of houses as they come. Our dad and his brothers were builders and I guess he learned from them.

After about 20 some years, he and Kathy, they split up and divorced. The girls, they both went on to school and earned degrees. Alisha has three kids: Katelyn, Tyler and Lily, the youngest, and Alice, she and her husband Colin have two kids: Isabel and Malachi. Well, Charlie, he remarried to a good woman, Shirley Brown, who had two kids, and Kathy, she remarried to Darren Stewart.

Me, I am not old enough to get married yet. Maybe someday, bah.

Grandfather Will Blankenship

Grandfather Will Blankenship was born in Flag Pond, Tennessee on November 11, 1879. He came from a large family, it was said; we really were not sure. He never talked of or about his family. The only one we were sure about was a brother named Arthur. He and his wife Laura and his brother Sparrel were killed in an auto train collision in 1917 in Kansas City, Missouri, and he had a brother, Jasper M born 1882, died 1891.

Will, he was a wandering man. He went west to Montana where he met my grandmother's brother Sam Parker. They were both herding sheep on the open prairie. It was there, when fall came and the sheep were brought in to the ranches that he and Sam decided to come back to North Carolina. During the last year herding sheep, he had been writing letters to a young lady named Cary Daily in North Carolina, and through these letters they had decided to get married.

Well, upon arriving in N.C., Sam, he directed Will to the home of Cary Daily where they met for the first time. She was not taken by Will and said so, and the wedding was called off. With nowhere else to go, he went home with Sam. When they arrived at Granny Parker's house and walked in, there sat my grandmother Bertha.

Well, Poppy, he looked at her and said "You are the girl I seen in my dreams."

They started courting, and after a short courtship they decided to get married, and did. They had five boys and three girls. Will, he started a store down at the forks of the road. For years he ran a successful business selling dry goods and local products.

After several years went by, the wild woods started calling him again. He bought traps, and every fall he would take off to the Nantahala River where he would spend the winter trapping for skins of all types. My Grandmother would keep us if we were sick and had to stay out of school. She would tell me stories about him trapping.

Well, one winter that he spent over there, he said it was unusually cold. He had built a small log house. It had no door on the sides, but instead it was located in the roof in one corner of the shack. One morning he ran the trap line. It was cold and snowing, the wind blowing out of the north colder than hell. He came in and cooked a small meal on the fireplace. He sat back, reading a little in a book he brought along. Well, being tired because his trap line was several miles long, he slept. Something kept waking him during the night, but he finally dozed off for good.

Next morning while checking the traps, one of them was thrown, but all he had was a claw from a cat. Well, as he checked his traps, one after the other was robbed. He started getting irritated and he figured it was the cat whose toe he caught. He made it back to the camp, ate his supper and went to bed.

Sometime late that night he felt something scratching at his covers. He laid real still and started thinking "what should I do?" Meanwhile, he was holding the covers over his self. After a few minutes of this, he came to a decision: he took a deep breath and hollered as loud as he could "SCAT THERE, TOM."

Well, that cat took half the roof off his little cabin. Poppy wasn't bothered the rest of the night. Next morning, when checking his traps, he had caught his cat; its toe was missing.

Dewey and Gertrude

Dewey, he was the quiet one of the Mull clan. He married Gertrude Nelson many years ago, and they built themselves a log house up in the cove right off of Tusquittee Creek. They had two girls as far as I know: one was Rachel, the other Effie May. Well, Rachel, she married one of the Saltz boys and moved to Vader, Washington. Effie, she was never married. She stayed with Dewey and Gert at home.

My Dad told me that when Dewey first got electric lights, he had one of them put in his barn. Well, the next morning, Dewey, he didn't have to have a lantern to milk by; instead he had the lights. Well, Gertrude, she saw Dewey turn on the light and take off to running as hard as he could. In a few minutes he would come walking back to the house. She asked what was going on; he said that every time he turned on the lights, that he couldn't run fast enough to see it come on.

Dewey, he said "That electricity shore was fast" 'cause he had run as fast as he could.

Gertrude, she said to Dewey "Why don't you let me turn on them lights and you go down to the barn and watch?"

She turned them on, and in a few minutes here he came.

She asked "What happened?"

He said "I seed it but don't believe it. Them there lights, they come on slicker then a button."

Dewey lived there most of his life and I don't think he ever had anything that used gasoline. They used a wood cook stove for food and a fireplace for heat. About every Sunday, Gertrude and Effie, they were at church, but I never did see Dewey there. I guess he made a little moonshine from time to time—just for medicine you understand—and Sundays was a good day. After church was over on Sunday, I would take Gert and Effie to the bottom of their driveway because my car wouldn't go up to the top.

They had a good life back in that cove of theirs. You never heard anything about their business and they didn't mind anyone else's. A few years later, Dewey, he passed on, but Gert and Effie, they stayed in the cove. They made their garden the same as before. They grew most of what they ate. In the summer they would pick blackberries and put them up. Effie would, in the fall, go to the woods and dig ginseng and May apple, among other herbs. She would also catch spring lizards.

They made it fine for years, and then Gertrude had a stroke and was partially paralyzed. Effie, she made her a pallet on the floor in front of the fireplace of their house. Gert said that she rested better on the floor where it was cooler. In the summer, Effie had to set and guard her mother, because the old log house, it had a fireplace built from rocks and mud. The mud had fallen out in places and the snakes had moved in; the copperheads were right at home in it. That first summer, Effie said that she killed 21 copperheads, with her just sitting in the old rocking chair. Them snakes would look for a warm place to sleep when dark came.

A few years later, Gertrude, she passed away and that left Effie by herself. She made do, I guess, and was probably a little lonesome. I would have been. Effie, she had good neighbors. Henry Mosteller, he would come check on her and also take her wherever she needed to go.

Well, one day Effie was picking blackberries when a copperhead bit her on the arm. Effie, being who she was, went back to the house and got out a pan, and poured into it vinegar and then poured into it a cup of table salt. She then soaked her arm in it.

The next day Henry came by, and saw her arm bandaged up and asked her what happened. She told him, and he loaded her into his truck and to the doctor they went. She got checked out, and the doc said she was fine; he could not have done any better.

That fall, her sister Rachel came and they sold the place. She loaded Effie up and to Washington State they went. The last time I heard, Effie was doing fine. I guess the home is where the heart is.

Luther Mull Barn

Luther Mull Corn Crib

Luther Mull's Cabin

Mull Family

The New Age of Bootlegging

The year is 1970 and things have changed a hundredfold. Most of the old timers have passed on, and a new age of moonshining has appeared. It is late in the afternoon; I am on my way to the Atlanta Airport to pick up a cousin who is on his way home from Viet Nam. He has been gone a year now and glad to be coming home. As we pull into the airport he is standing out front ready to go.

We get started coming up I -75, and he says "I need to borrow a few clothes for a few days."

I tell him OK, but what happened to his? He says that he didn't have room for them. Well, he opens his duffel bag and pulls out something that would change everyone's life for a few years to come. The duffel is full of thai sticks—marijuana in dried form. Oh, we did not even comprehend what would take place after that!

Well, when we got home the next day, where the night went I will never know. We smoked us some and got to talking about the war, among other things. We ran across some seeds in the sticks, and, well, me being raised a farmer, I kept a few. The next week I planted a handful.

We planted every last one of them seeds. I would go back every few days and check on them. After about six weeks I knew we were in big trouble. That stuff was growing at the rate of about a foot a week. In three months it was at least 12 feet tall and still growing. I had never seen anything grow so tall so fast!

Fall came and we cut our plants. We had quite a few, but it didn't seem to be as strong as the stuff he brought home from 'Nam. Meanwhile, we had started hanging out in Hiawassee, GA on the weekends. My cousin had a few friends from 'Nam that lived over there, and I guess they had the same idea about growing as we did. They had a few seeds that they saved and we did a little trading.

Well, the next spring we went to the woods again. We dug holes in the ivy thickets, built a chicken wire fence to keep out the varmints, and then we dug a hole a little bigger than a five gallon bucket. We carried cow manure to the holes and mixed it with the dirt, got a few real soggy corn cobs from the hog pen and placed them in the bottom of the hole. That way, if it was a dry summer, the cobs would hold water every time it rained, and help get the plants through the dry spell.

Well, when they started to bloom or make tops we would take the pollen from those Georgia plants, and dust our plants there for cross pollinating into a new strain of pot. Well, that fall it turned out a little stronger than the last year's crop, but it still was not as strong as the original. For years after that we kept cross-pollinating these things. A few years later it started to catch on and EVERYONE started to grow the stuff; there was money to be made and it was easier than making moonshine and even the folks that made "moon" were growing!

In the years that followed, I guess it kind of got out of hand. It turned out to be the leading money crop in the state, surpassing tobacco and corn. Then came the little white airplane.

That sucker, you could spot it for a half mile. The first year they found tons and tons of it; it was growing everywhere! Of course no one was tending it and they said it had started growing wild. This brought out a different kind of grower. Now that they had the plane and the National Guard to help, it was harder to get by with.

I do know that some of the forest service personnel would ride in the choppers and help to spot it and not say anything. After they quit for the day they would sneak in and pull it for themselves. This happened a lot of times.

Because the hills have eyes, this prompted a new type of security. The growers would go into a laurel thicket and tie the limbs back so they could get sun to the plants. They could leave them back until the plane started flying, and then cut the strings and the laurels closed back over them. All they had to do was read the paper, which always told when the plane was coming.

Well, this went on for years, with everyone getting a piece. The forest service would look for a trail just the same as the revenuers would years before while looking for stills. Well, there is a way around that: you go in and take out the male plants. This way there is no pollination and you come up with sensimilla which is seedless and all buds. Someone came up with the idea of burying a water line to the hills. That way you don't leave a trail to it, thus you have camouflage until harvest time.

Well, if anybody has the idea of growing this stuff, think again. If you are CAUGHT you will serve time in JAIL. After all these years and a lot of culturing, the southeast has some of the most potent pot in the world. I personally think that the war in Vietnam caused a lot of things that hurt our world here in the mountain. Not that it wouldn't have eventually happened anyway, but a lot of our boys were sent home wounded and never had any help getting off the drugs they were on. Sorry, guys. We owe ya' all a whole lotta thanks, for what it is worth.

Steve and Zadie Rowland

Steve and Zadie were married at a very young age. They loaded their belongings on a wagon pulled by a team of horses, and headed for the Burch Cove. After arriving, they started building a house, and set up to housekeeping as any young couple would. From the start, they had just enough to get by while living in the Burch Cove. Steve, he made a living like anyone else; he worked some at the sawmill, and sometimes he made moonshine.

While living there, they had four kids: Stella, Martha, Ruth and Vierce. Later on, they moved to the Morgan Branch about a mile from the first homestead. There, three more kids were conceived. These were Cloey, Wilma and Elveta. Well, Zadie, she would send the girls Veta and Wilma to gather the eggs.

Veta said her and Wilma were playing in the sawdust pile hiding the eggs one day, and when time to go home came, they went to looking for the eggs and couldn't find them. Well, when they got home, Zadie asked about the eggs, and Veta, she said they had to lie and tell her the chickens hadn't laid any. That didn't go over too good with Zadie.

The eggs meant they had something to eat, for back then you had to raise or grow about everything you ate. It was a long ways to the store and when you got there all they had was dry goods and the staples such as flour, salt, and spices. They had no coolers for milk or soda pops, which they could not afford anyway. Back then, they traded for the things they didn't have, which were things other people had traded in on products they did not have or grow.

Most folks would load up on Saturday and take their corn and wheat to the grist mill, which was located at the fork of the road. They could get it ground for a portion of the product. For example, for grinding a bushel of flour or meal, the mill person would take a couple of scoops for toll. They would grow all their vegetables and some folks grew sugar cane. When harvest time came they would cut the fodder off the stalks, then cut the cane and take it to Syrup Mill Hill, which was on Lick Log.

There they would turn it over to Burgen and Bonnie Parker. Burgen would grind it into pulp, then Bonnie, she would take the juice and cook it into sorghum syrup. They would store it in syrup jugs. These jugs were made of clay and held about two gallons. All winter long, the sorghum was used for cooking or making of moonshine, or, in most cases, it was taken to school by the kids for their lunch.

My dad said they would take a gallon bucket and a cake of corn pone. At lunch time all the kids would gather around the eldest brother or sister and eat sorghum and corn pone. This practice brought on the term of carrying a lunch bucket.

When the next fall came, if there was any sorghum left when the new crop was harvested, last year's was used for making moonshine; it took the place of sugar. In the fall, they also had candy pulls and candy bitings. That was where all the kids of the area gathered, they would cook the syrup into taffy, then the boys would put a piece in their mouth and the girl of his choice would put the other end in her mouth and they would eat until it was gone.

When my great grandfather first came here, he said that when he came up Cold Branch, he was almost to the gap in the mountain, and he said you could look to your right and all you could see was white on the hillside. They went over to see what it was; it turned out to be feathers dropped when the Indians were forced to move along the Trail of Tears which would end up in Oklahoma.

Grandfather settled on land at the mouth of Nan Branch and I still live there today on the same spot the Indians were forced to leave what they could not carry, which was their feather ticks which were in their mattresses and their pillows. They did not want the white men to have them, so they tore them open and scattered the feathers.

They also had an Indian marble ground where they played games such as marbles, foot races, wrestling and so on. It is now used for making moonshine, occasionally.

This place is located just under the Stamey Nob, and will remain untouched because I now own it. You can see where it was; it is like a dry pond on the side of the mountain. Tusquittee has many creeks running into it; if you start at the top and come down the left side there is Perry Mill Creek, Hurricane Creek, Chairmaker, Cold Branch, Gudge Branch, Stamey Cove Creek, Downings Creek, and on the right you have Tuni Creek, Compass Cothren Branch, Johnson Creek, and Bristol Branch.

Anyway, Steve and Zadie had thought about starting their homestead here, but since it was already taken and there was no reason to crowd anybody, they moved on and settled in Burch Cove. It worked out real well for them for a while, until they settled for good on Morgan Branch. With so much water in this area, there was always the right place for everyone, and no one had to fight for a homestead. They was always a way for folks to make their own.

Joe and Muriel Blankenship

Willis Joe Blankenship was born July 21, 1924 on Cold Branch Road. He spent most of his youth right here. When they were growing up, it was pretty tough times. The depression was in full swing and times were really hard. He told me that he and his brothers and sisters helped to grow everything they ate.

They would walk to school, which was located on upper Tusquittee. That meant they had to walk about four miles each way, as the school was located where Ray Stillwell has his home today. Dad said they would start walking at 6:00 in the morning to be to school on time.

They would walk up the Nelson Ridge Road about a mile, then down Chairmaker Branch which runs into Tusquittee Creek, then up the creek to the school house. Upon getting to school, their teacher was Roy Gibson. They went there for several years and then the school was moved to Chigger Hill, which is at the mouth of Downing's Creek.

Well, my dad went there until the eighth grade. When he turned 16 years old he worked at Fontana on the dam helping to build it. He said that was where he bought his first car for the grand sum of $50.00. It was a 1932 Ford coupe and was black in color. On his way home with it he was stopped by the cops in Andrews. He didn't have a license, but they let him go anyway.

Dad said that he would haul moonshine across Tuni Mountain over to Junaluska Creek, and if they ran out of gas on the way they would stop and pour in a gallon of shine! The mountain was pretty steep up toward the top, and sometimes he would have to turn around and go up backwards because the carburetor was fed gas with gravity.

When he turned 17, he was off to Florida where he welded on ships that were used in World War II. He worked in Panama City for a year working 50 feet above the water. He worked mainly with women workers, because the men were all at war.

At 18 years old he was drafted and sent to Fort Bragg, North Carolina for six weeks of basic training. When he was drafted, so was his first cousin Sammy Allison. They were both sent to Bragg.

When they were sent to war, Sammy went to Europe and Dad was sent to the Pacific. His first stop was the Hawaiian Islands and for the next few years he made his way to Tokyo, Japan the hard way. He was an engineer in the army, and the engineers, they went in front of the army and built the bridges and roads or repaired the existing ones. He said that the guys on the machines would get shot and the next one in the chow line was next to go. He would work until his turn came or was shot, then the next guy would take his turn.

When they got to Tokyo, he said that there was nothing left standing but the steel beams of the buildings; the concrete was blown away. He stayed there for a while until his time was up, then it was back to California. The trip lasted for 31 days. They were fed powdered eggs and no bread, just eggs. They were 2500 men on a converted cattle freighter. The puck was ankle deep and the seas didn't cooperate.

Now, my mom, she had it pretty rough growing up back home, to find there were no jobs to be had. It was tough times here. Dad loaded up and off to Ohio he went, where he worked for Timken Roller Bearing for a while, and then decided he needed to get home.

When he got home, he bought him a '40 Ford coupe. Guess he was quite the young man back in his day, running around in his fancy car. He went with a few girls and then one day he ran into my mom.

They courted for a pretty good while, then snuck off and got hitched. Well, the first night they were together they stayed at her mom's house. Dad's mom, she got worried about where he was so she sent his brother to find him. When she found out that he was married she went to happy!

Well, they built a house, it was 1946. Dad had asked would she druther have a house or a ring, she chose the house. Now, my mom, she had it pretty rough growing up. She was born in Haverhill, Massachusetts. When she was three years old, her mom and dad moved down here with six kids.

Grandpa Doyle, he wasn't much for working and did as little as possible. He did work for Lawrence Ellis at his sawmill for a little while, then he went back to New York. When he got there he went to work for the Italian mafia. I guess they were not very nice people from what I could gather.

After a while he would show up here again. Well, gramps and granny, they had two more kids in the years that followed. I guess it was pretty hard for granny and the eight kids because the Great Depression was in full swing. Mom said that they would work all day for something to eat, be it a gallon of milk or a peck of fruit, it didn't much matter. They went to Elf Elementary school and lived on the creek below Stanoke Ledford's store.

In 1939, the TVA, they wanted to build a dam and back up the river. Well, Mom's Uncle George Spurr, he said that he wasn't going to move and they couldn't make him. They started the dam, and, George, he didn't budge until one day the water was backed up to the front porch. I guess old Unc, he had to pack up pretty quick and get out. The TVA, they moved them and my grandmother. George built a house on for himself on old Highway 64 and one for my granny on Burnt Schoolhouse Ridge where it still stands today.

Well, Grandpa, he went north again and never came back. Years later he was buried in Glens Falls New York. He had left his wife and kids to raise themselves and they did so with the help of neighbors and friends. They were raised very poor and had very little, but they did the best they could with what they had. A lot of people looked down on them because they were poor and didn't have the nicer things. They wore hand-me-downs and ate what they could raise or work out. Mom always said that you wouldn't miss what you never had in the first place.

Dad and mom, they had four of us kids and I guess I was the black sheep of the family, but even I finally came around to momma's way of thinking. We never had too much but I do have something that most of you people will never have: I HAVE ENOUGH OF EVERYTHING.

Meat house and corn crib @ Blankenships

Joe Blankenship as a young man

Muriel Blankenship as a young woman

Speedy Guffey

Speedy, he was a character and should have been born a hundred years ago. Instead, he was born around 1940 and was the eldest of five kids. He was a little wild from the start. We called him Speedy because he would move so slow and methodically, he knew his every move before he made it.

Well, Speed, he went to school for a few years, but I don't think he went all the way. When young, he learned to make moonshine and he was pretty good at it. He was married four or five times and had a passel of kids—the one thing he was good at. He loved horses and would use them to carry everything he needed to the woods.

When he married the last wife it was questioned by the authorities. He was asked if he had ever divorced his first four wives.

He said "What's a divorce?"

They explained to him what bigamy was and charged him with it. Well, instead of going to court he went to the woods on his big black horse. The law, they looked for him for years but he was always one step ahead of them. Seven years passed and the statute of limitations took effect and the charges were dropped.

Speed, he went west to Montana to the ranch that belonged to Big John Gribble.

Big John had married into the Sioux Indian tribe and his ranch was on the reservation. The only law on the reservation was the Indian police. Well, Speedy, he was right at home there. He worked the ranch and was paid a cowhand's wages. He worked there several years before he moved to the state of Washington where two sisters lived.

Speed went to a bar in town and was having a drink at the bar when a guy came over to him and sat down on the barstool next to him. Well, he reached over and grabbed Speed's cowboy hat off his head. Speedy got his hat back and he said to the guy "Don't bother my hat."

Well, the drunk, he reached over and grabbed it again. Speedy reached inside his coat, pulled out his .38 Special and shot him, then said "I told you not to take my hat."

This put Speedy on the run again. A few weeks later he showed up on Tusquittee, and it was back to the woods again where he stayed seven more years. Well, time passed, the charges were dropped and Speedy, he was free again. He married once again and this time it was legally done. He built him a house out of logs that he cut off his dad's place. It was way back up in the hollow. There he sired his last kid. It was a boy and he named him after Jesse James.

Well, Speedy, he and his wife, they lived there many years. Every year they would go to Montana, where they would hunt deer and elk. She would can the meat, and back home they would come. The folks around, they didn't bother Speedy. He was a real good neighbor, never bothering anyone and always helped if you needed it. His wife, she was a very nice lady and mother.

Nineteen eighty three, it rolled around and it was the first year that the law flew its airplane. Speedy and his wife were gone hunting again. I had noticed he had planted what looked like trees in his garden; you could see them from the road when the leaves were off. That plane started flying and we noticed it kept circling over Speedy's house. Down the road came a bunch of law cars; they turned and went over to Speedy's. Well, it turned out that Speedy was in trouble again. They found about 52 huge pot plants in his garden and a bunch more in an outbuilding. It was enough to be charged with a felony.

While all this was taking place, Speedy and his family were still in Montana hunting. The sheriff nailed a letter on his door, and when he came home two months later, it was back to jail. His wife bailed him out when court was over. Speedy, he was sentenced to 144 days in county jail and the fines we will probably never know; it was a bunch.

He served his time, and, I think, learned a lesson. Today he sits in his wheel chair and lives in his cabin. Still, he's got no electric power, no phone, no hot water, but is as happy as anyone I know of. He lives a hundred years behind us but you know, I believe he is richer than most folks and hasn't a care in the world. WE SHOULD ALL BE THIS WAY, IT WOULD BE A BETTER WORLD! WE ARE TRULY SPOILED.

The Olympic Park Bomber, Eric Robert Rudolph

Eric Rudolph was said to be the Olympic Park Bomber, but some of us folks have our doubts. This guy was said to have blown up several different places. Well, us folks around here don't believe he did all of them. He was said to have been tied to several different militia groups. As a matter of fact, they is six or eight different groups in and around Cherokee County.

Anyway, he was singled out as the one that did it. I am not saying that he did it or did not do it, but it seems to me that there had to be more than one man involved. This man was called guilty long before he was caught, and in this country I thought that a person was innocent until proven guilty. I guess not in this case. The FBI wanted to put a lid on this thing before it got away.

Anyone who knows anything at all about these here Tusquittee Mountains knows that anyone who knows his or her way around could hide in them for as long as they please. Eric, he was pretty smart when it came to hiding out in the mountains, the simple reason being he was in the armed forces.

As a matter of fact, he was in the 82nd Airborne. Now, this branch of the service required a whole bunch of gorilla training, which included mountain training and survival. Well now, anyone that has been raised around here could survive in the woods by living off the land. The FBI, they don't want to admit that they were outclassed by an old mountain man. Old Rudolph, he led them around by the nose like they was rookies. He had his connections in and around Andrews and the areas around there.

The biggest problem the FBI had was that they knew too much about these here mountains. Now, my dad, he always said that the biggest fool in the world was the educated one. In this case it seemed so, huh.

When old Rudolph got back to Andrews he put together what supplies he thought he needed, and to the mountains he went. But the first year he wasn't always in the woods where the Feds were looking. I know on several occasions he was seen at some of his friend's funerals; this was on two occasions. Then one time I saw him myself at the hardware store in Hayesville. Then the search picked up the pace, and he went to the woods and stayed for a while.

Well, the only problem was that there are a lot of woods around here; if you don't think so just go up to the Tusquitee Bald and have a look. Now, when we were teenagers we would go up there and stay for two weeks and deer hunt. A person can go up Fires Creek and look around and see it is a pretty big place. There is a place called the Rock House up there and from it you can see all of Andrews, including where the FBI headquarters was located.

One night, the school kids from Murphy High School were having a graduation party at the Bob Allison Campground up on Tuni Creek. Now, everyone knows what their party must have been like, because we were all teenagers at one time or another. Well, they were all having a good old time, had a bonfire and coolers full of beer, and—knowing the kids—a little moonshine to prevent catching a cold, and probably a few joints of weed.

Well, about midnight, a guy dressed in camouflage walked up to the fire and started warming his hands. Of course he had a few beers and a few tokes off a joint, then helped himself to some food and had a good old time for a while. Then he just vanished into the night. Well now, nobody thought much of it until one of the kids was walking through her parent's kitchen the next morning. Her folks were watching the T.V. When she looked at it, she saw the guy that had been at their party the night before and said to her parents "That man was at our graduation party last night."

Her father called the FBI and the search was on again with much more force. Old Rudolph, he had come down Tuni Creek from the Signal Bald. To say the least, the FBI was furious that he had slipped through their fingers again. They set up the search in grids and went to looking again. They contacted Rudolph's old commanding officer from the military and asked him what he would do, and he told them that if Old Rudolph wanted to be found it would happen, and if he didn't want to they were wasting their time. He said that this guy could hide from them in 40 acres and he was in 40,000, so they had little chance of catching him.

Little did they know he had outsmarted them again: he moved his living quarters again. One day I came home from work, pulled into my dad's driveway and guess who was there? The FBI. They were asking my old man if he had seen Rudolph. Well, when my dad said "Yep I seed him," they got all excited and asked where. He said "On the TV."

Well now, that man's face lit up like a candle and Dad, he just grinned real big and his gold tooth was just a-shinin'. Now, that FBI man, he had met his match when he met my dad. He asked Dad what he would do if Rudolph came to his house and asked for food.

Well, Dad, he said "I would feed him and give him a bed for the night and send him on his way in the morning."

That FBI man, he just looked at Dad and said "Would that not be harboring a criminal?"

Dad, he just looked at him and said "He ain't went to trial yet and ain't a man innocent until proven guilty?"

Well, they pulled out and left Cold Branch and everything settled down for a time.

Meanwhile, one of our neighbors, Tinnie Mosteller, her health turned for the worst, and her daughter had her put into the care center in Hayesville. The daughter, she lives in the state of Oregon and she wanted me to look after her mom's house, so we went and we boarded up the windows and locked all of the doors. We went through the house and checked out things. In the kitchen was about two hundred jars of food she had canned. Out on the back porch was the well, so we locked her down and agreed to look in on occasion.

Well, that summer it was hot. Every day I had to drive by her house on my way home from work. The house was only about 30 feet from the road but the kudzu, it growed and completely covered the house. Now, in the summer it was almighty snakey because we have lots of copperheads on Cold Branch and I wasn't about to go into that old house.

One day my neighbor stopped by and told me that the front door was open, so I went up there and looked in that old house. Well, you ain't going to believe what I found when I went into the kitchen: they weren't a jar of food left on the shelf that had anything in it, the back door was open and they was a bucket in the well. In the bedroom on the back of the house it was a mess, looking like someone had been using it for a long time, probably most of the summer. The only thing missing was the food from the pantry. Nothing else was bothered.

Well, I set into thinking, now who would have been living here, and it didn't take long to decide who it was. I closed the doors and locked them again and went back to my dad's house and who do you think was there when I drove into the yard? My friends from the FBI. This time they started to question me and asked if I had seen Rudolph. Well, I said I had, and they ask where, and I told them on the TV.

Well, that feller's face, it got cherry red and then I thought it best that I told them about the old house of Tinnie's. They all jumped in their cars and up the road they went. For several days after that we saw their men walking in the woods around the house, but no Rudolph. Finally they left and started to look elsewhere. About a year later they caught him in Murphy and to this day I believe that it was him who stayed in the old house.

And there is one thing about it: if he had not wanted to be caught and was not tired of running, he would still be running loose. I guess he has a permanent home in Colorado at the federal prison now. I guess for him it was a good run and he had them fooled for a long time. And the FBI, they were just outclassed by an old mountain man.

Randall and Ula May McAllister

Randall and Ula May were a mismatched couple, and how and why they ever got together is a miracle. Anyway, it happened and some good things did come of their marriage. They had a whole passel of girls, and fine girls they were. The eldest was Peggy, she was a beautiful girl. Then there was Lulu or Lucretia, then came Sharon (she was a wild one) then Darlene (she was the cute one), then Jackie (she was the serious one), then came Lahoma, who was the quiet one.

I am not really sure how long Randall and Ula May were together, but when I got to know the girls they were not together anymore. Anyway, they lived up on the hill above the Tusquittee Church in an old house. The driveway was real rough, so most people would park down at the road and walk up a path to the house.

Well, Peggy the eldest, she married pretty young to one of the Byers boys from the Carter Cove section of Clay County. I think it was Roy Lee and they had a baby. But when it was still real young, Peggy, she was shot and killed. Well, Randall, he swore that he would make it right, but at the time I think he was in prison. Well, Lulu, she married Aaron Martin and moved to town, where in later years they opened and operated a grocery store.

Now that brings us to Sharon. She married Louie Ledford and moved to Shooting Creek, where they had several kids. Then in later years they divorced. Louie, he was a little feller, but when he got drunk on moonshine he turned mean and would always find a woman to beat on. Now, Sharon being a McAllister—which is Black Irish—they take no crap from anyone. She would whoop him like a dog. Finally she got smart and left him.

Fast forward to 1977, and things have changed a whole lot. Last night we had our first killing frost and it's now time to harvest the crop. It has been a perfect year to grow and the buds are exceptionally large. I have already taken in some buds that will dry out to a quarter of a pound each. It's been a week and all of the crop is in, with the exception of one at the end of the Burch Cove road. There is a large clear cut there and the dirt is perfect for growing.

Everything goes well until the sheriff and his deputies find the crop. Hartsell Moore is the sheriff, and his deputies are Felix Lance, Larry Sellers and Narvel Garrett. They have been taking turns watching the patch, and have been there for about a week. In a case like this, you have to do some thinking. It so happened that we were having a party on Perry Mill Creek that Saturday night and three of the McAllister girls were there and what a party it was! Everyone was drinking a few beers, along with a little moonshine and smoking a lot of pot. I guess when you get just enough in you a man will do most anything to impress the girls.

We had seen Felix going in for his shift watching that patch of smoke, and it was around midnight. The moon was full and what better time to harvest. Everyone was passed out, so I took out up Perry Creek with a canvas duffel bag; it was one of the kind the soldiers use. It was only about two miles to the patch, and when I got there, sure enough, there was Felix sitting in his car watching that patch.

Well, I set out to crawling to that patch. Now, Felix was about 150 yards above it. That clear cut was anything but clear! It took about an hour of crawling, all the while watching Felix moving when he would doze off for a few zzzz's. In a little while, the moon, it started to set and the time was right. I took that pot right out from under his nose, and I mean every little bit of it. I have always wondered what the sheriff said to Felix the next morning. I bet it was plenty.

I started dating Jackie McAllister, and of course we had a lot of parties. We dated for several months and then they moved into my trailer house up on the hill. It was Jackie, Darlene and their Uncle Danny. We called him by his nickname, which was Boon. They lived there for a while, and then one night it snowed a lot. Well, we started playing poker and after a while it turned into strip poker. I am not going into details but it got pretty wild and somehow I woke up in bed with Darlene. We were together for a while and then one day, for some reason she took off with someone else. Well, that ended a party that lasted well over a year.

I didn't see any of them for a long time, because two weeks later I took off for the west coast. I intended to stay for a couple of weeks and ended up staying for five years. After that, I never got in a hurry again, life's too short. But a few things turned out for the good. While gone, I quit alcohol, cigarettes and pot, so it was worth it a hundred times over. Years, they have passed and every once in a while I see one of the sisters and a man always thinks back and says what if ?

Grandmother Bertha Parker Blankenship and Poppy

Grandma Bertha, she was a God fearing person. Every time the doors of the church opened, she was waiting. She was a member of the Tusquittee Church of God and could have preached if she'd had a mind to.

She was born on May 14, 1890 on Buck Creek. Her father, Alfred Parker, moved to Cold Branch around the turn of the century. He settled on the mouth of the Nan Branch where he owned most of it. He had come from the Buck Creek area on the other side of Chunkie Gal Mountain, the east slope. Like all pioneers, he decided to "go west" and ended up in what is now known as the Cold Branch Community in the township of Tusquitteee.

Well, Grandma Bertha, she had five boys and three girls. When anyone got down sick, they would holler for Grandma and she would go and take care of them. It didn't matter how long it took or what was required of her. I remember when we were kids, if we were sick and could not go to school, my dad would take us to her house so he and mom could go to work. While there, she would tell me stories about when she and Poppy were young. My grandfather died when I was two years old so I didn't remember him.

This is how it was told to me. While herding sheep in Montana, the summers were long and the nights were short. Every couple of days he had to move the herd. He had about 2000 head to take care of. With this many sheep you had plenty of problems to contend with: one was enough water, and then you had to have grass for them.

Well, with that many sheep you had to have help, so he had two dogs. I guess the largest problem was with the wolves; they were stalking the herd constantly. Coyotes were also a problem, but the dogs could handle them pretty well. They had supplies brought to them by the owner of the sheep. If they ran short they ate mutton.

When fall came, they would drive the sheep back to the ranch for the winter. Poppy and the dogs would stay behind and make sure that all the animals made it to the ranch. The day after they came for the sheep, Poppy and his dogs were out looking for strays, when he noticed a couple of wolves following at a distance. He had slaughtered a sheep that morning. Of course there was blood, and the wolves, having smelled it, were looking for the source.

Poppy, he came back to the wagon where he lived. This wagon was built out of wood and boxed in solid. It had a small stove in one end where he cooked in bad weather. Darkness came, the wolves started howling, and his dogs that normally slept outside started scratching at the door wanting in. Well, he could hear the wolves; they were real close, so he let his dogs in.

The wolves had found where he killed the sheep and were fighting over the remains. Poppy, he had a 30.06 rifle. He could see them fighting out a small window in the door. He shot a wolf. Instantly, the others jumped on it and it was torn to pieces. Poppy, he shot again, the same thing happened. Well, by then, other wolves had came to the feast. He kept shooting until he ran out of shells.

Well, it was a waiting game then. By the next morning come daylight, the wolves were gone. The rancher, he came with a team to take the wagon back to the ranch. They had survived one hell of a night.

Another time when Poppy was returning to the ranch, he came to the Missouri River where they had built a bridge from two trees. He started across with his horse behind him, and was about halfway there when a silvertip grizzly showed up at the other end. He had his rifle and shot the bear until all his bullets were gone. He then got on that horse and got outta there!

He went to town the next day. Well, on his way back to the ranch, there at the footbridge—where he stood while shooting—laid that Grizzly. He made sure it was dead, then he cut its scalp off, and, when in town the next trip, he sold it for $50 bounty.

Great Grandpa Alfred Parker

Granny Muriel Blankenship

My mom in the last six years has been through a lot. Back in 2004, my dad, he passed away and it had to be hard for her. They had been married for 56 years and all at once she was alone. I know it was a lot to get used to and she did. Without any complaints.

I lived up on the hill above her and my dad. Six months before he passed, I came down to live with them, mainly because I didn't have a phone and he was sick a lot. Within one week I had to take him to the emergency room because he could not breathe. Well, when he passed, I stayed on with my mom mostly to keep her company because she had not been alone for over 50 years.

Well, after a few years, a friend of mine and I decided to take a little trip out west and go elk hunting for a few weeks. My friend Jack Dorman and I left for Hanna, Utah in October of 2008. We left on the morning of the 15th and were going to stop in Hanna for a week, and then on to Washington state for elk season.

Well, we spent six days in Hanna, and on the afternoon of the seventh day I got a phone call; my mom was in the hospital in Gainesville, Georgia and was going to have heart surgery. I asked Mike, whose home we were staying at, if he could make flight arrangements for the following day. This he did. Well, the next morning Jack and I loaded up and headed for Salt Lake City, Utah where I caught a flight for Atlanta, Georgia. That afternoon I landed in Hartsville Jackson, and 30 minutes later my older brother Henry landed.

Upon arriving in Gainesville, we met with the doctor, and he told us this was a unique case. He had asked my mom when was the last time she was to the doctor's, and she said that it was 29 years ago. Then he asked her when was the last time she was in the hospital and she said in 1946, that was when she was in a school bus accident coming home from school. Well, you should have seen that doc's face!

They did surgery and did a triple bypass on her heart. When we next seen her, she was wrapped up like a little cocoon. She was in intensive care for about five days and then in a regular room for a few more. Then it was time for home.

Well, my older brother and I, we would take turns setting up with her. This lasted for a couple of weeks. The rate of improvement was unreal. Within a month she was on her feet and agoin', not too fast at first, but as the weeks went on she got faster. At the end of three months, she was going about three-quarter speed and getting faster every week.

Well, its spring now, and Granny, she is back to full speed and is working the garden, which we downsized a little bit; she has only about an acre now. She has a tater patch that is about a quarter of an acre. She went back to the doctor last week and he told her that her days of hoeing the garden was about over and she should take it a little easier. This is a hard thing to do because she is a little stubborn about slowing down.

Well, Charlie and I, we do all of the hoeing now, and she does the gathering of vegetables, and the canning. Last year she put up about 80 cans of green beans and a whole bunch of sweet corn, greens, mustard, okra and, of course, maters and taters, which we had about 15 bushels of.

She had her chickens until about a month ago when I was awakened in the wee hours of the morning to the sound of chickens a-squawkin'. I got my light and went to see; they were 13 laying there dead and I wondered what in the world had happened. At 5:00 the next morning, I went back over and they were 24 dead. Only two were left alive.

Well, I got one of my live traps and put the two live ones in it. The next evening I placed them in the trap on the floor of the chicken house, and beside of them I placed another trap. The next morning I had caught a mink; he was solid black. That thing had, in about three hours, cut the throats of all of her chickens and did not eat any of them. Now that's coldblooded.

Well, Granny, she was disappointed, but the chickens will be replaced real soon. Meanwhile she has been making quilts with her sister Ann and they are something to see. They spend most of the day quilting. I guess this is a good pastime for them and it makes them a little spending money.

I think that everything will return to normal pretty soon. On her next birthday she will turn 85 years young. I just hope I can keep up with her. She is an incredible human being; she is up every day at 5:00 and goes until dark. Some people say I should slow her down, but I think she is old enough to make up her own mind, and it would do little good to say anything anyway. All I have to say is: do what you want to do and go where you want to go.

Joe and Muriel Blankenship Homestead

The Killian Brothers: Smellit and Chillie

The Killian brothers were about the best neighbors a person could ever ask for. This story starts with the younger of the two; we nicknamed him Smellit, because every time he started to eat anything he had to smell of it.

Smellit, he would come to our house to hang out with us boys. He was pretty bad to curse, and my mom would take him aside and tell him that if he cursed around us kids she would send him home. He was about five years older than we were.

Well, he came regular until he turned 16 years old, then his interest changed to the girls. They were not many jobs then, so he did what about everyone else did and that was to make a little whiskey.

Well, he teamed up with one of his buddies and they set up a still. It was kind of ironic because the name of the branch his folks lived on was Stillhouse Branch. Well, Smellit and his friend set them up a still and made liquor. They did real good at it for a while.

At least one night a week you would hear Smellit fire up his old 1962 Chevy. That old car had a 409 big block V8, with no mufflers, so when he started her up everyone would start looking for their kids and get them out of the road. Smellit, he was not the best driver on the road anyway. Well, you could set your clock by when he would haul a load.

Well, one night while carrying out a load which was six gallons, they ran into a surprise. They didn't get but about one quarter of a mile from the still when the law was waiting for them. Well, Smellit, he threw his load down over a rock cliff; he later showed me where it was when we were deer hunting on that mountain. There didn't seem any way a glass jug could survive that toss. Well, it busted one jug and left five for evidence. They both were taken to jail and were tried in court. They both were to serve 18 months in Petersburg federal prison. I believe that taught Smellit a lesson about making moonshine.

Well, the years passed and Smellit, he kept a real job. At first he did a little carpentry work, and then he found a job in Wyoming building aqueducts for hydroelectric power plants and worked at them for years.

Finally, he came back to North Carolina and semi-retired. I guess he saved him some money and made a nice home for himself. There he lived to the ripe old age of 47. I guess he had a heart attack and did not survive. All in all, he had full life and lived it like he wanted. We buried Smellit at the little chapel on Rainbow Springs alongside his father who had lived to the age of 100 years.

Chillie was the older of the Killian brothers. He was about the best maker of moonshine that ever came off Tusquittee. Well, old Chillie, he would sneak around and make a little moonshine from time to time. That came to an abrupt end one day when he was in his stillhouse.

Unknown to Chillie, he was being watched by some folks that didn't take too much to moonshiners. The day came when they caught Chillie in the act of making a little shine. This meant one thing and that was a free vacation at the federal prison.

Well now, Chillie, he had him an old 1949 Ford car and a nice one it was. It was black and a two-door coupe. Well, his brother Smellit, he jacked it up on blocks while his brother was away in prison. I am not real sure how long he was gone but it was for a while and it was long enough that the engine stuck. Well, Chillie, he got out of prison and he sold the old car to the junk yard owned by Sam Cox just out of Hayesville.

Well, the people who were native to this county know where the junk yard was and who Sam Cox was. My dad, he sent my brother Henry out to Sam's to buy that old car and after a long time he made that thing run. Sam, he wanted $50 for that old car, but Henry being the wheeler dealer he was, got it for $35.

Well, back to Chillie. He was out of jail for a while, and then he had some trouble come up, and back to the prison he went. It was for probation violation this time and away he went and paid his debt to society once again. This time he decided he'd had enough and from then on changed his ways.

Well, it wasn't long until he married Fanny Stillwell Parker. This was a match that was meant to be, for they were married for a lot of years. Fanny, she was a little older than Chillie and I think this helped to tame Old Chillie down a little bit.

After being married for a few years, they had a son they named Mike, and he too turned out to be a fine man. Mike, he was a quiet type fellow and never bothered anyone that I know of. I know that when he got out of school, after a few years he went to the state of Alaska where he was the Captain of an ocean going tug boat, and run it on the Yukon river for many years and was good at his job. Years later he came back home to Tusquittee.

Now, old Chillie, after he got home the second time, he got him a job working for Pike Electric company and did this for years. When he retired and was back home, he thought he would try making a little moonshine just so he would not forget how. Well, the revenuers found out about it again and here they come again. Well, they came into the house and they found nothing. They looked everywhere and no still. Old Chillie had outsmarted them this time.

Well, they kept an eye on him and knew he was making, but could not catch him in the act, and never did after that. One day they came back to check on Chillie. Well, his wife Fanny was canning vegetables, the kitchen was hotter than hell, and it was ninety degrees outside.

Chillie, he didn't know they were there and was trying to get out of a hidden cellar under the house. They were standing on the trap door hidden under a mat on the floor. Well, they left a little later.

Chillie came up out of there mad as heck until he found out why the door wouldn't open. I guess he had run a stove pipe up behind his wife's wood stove and hooked the pipes together and out the roof. Well, when you saw smoke coming out the stove pipe you could bet Chillie was working.

Well, he quit all that illegal stuff years ago. Now he still lives where he and Fanny lived for most of their married years. Fanny, she passed away a few years ago and is truly missed by everyone around. What I remember most of all is when I would be coming home from work and driving up Tusquittee, I would pass Chillie and Fanny's house, and if it was warm weather they would be sitting on the front porch and you would always see that little hand a-waving and she was always smiling.

Chillie, he still lives in the same place and I see him driving up or down Cold Branch about every day. And if there is one thing you can count on, it's that he will always wave.

Spunk and Dee Mosteller

Spunk—whose real name was Donald—was born and raised on Tusquittee and so was his wife Dee. Both were raised in the same community about a half mile apart. They were married young, and then times were very hard.

They had an old house up on the hill above Spunk's dad Bud. I know that Spunk had a brother named Paul but everyone called him Root. Now, Root, he made a little moonshine and so did Spunk. Root, he made his moon in one holler, and Spunk, he would go up another.

Now, Spunk, he would work wherever he could find work and the jobs were hard to find back then, so he would have to make a little moonshine to make ends meet. Back then everyone was making "moon" and the competition was fierce. I guess that the sheriff found out about Spunk and Root making liquor.

Root, he decided to pull out and he left the county. He loaded his family and moved to Washington State to look for work.

Spunk, he went back to making liquor, and I guess the sheriff at the time, Neil Kitchens, he came to Spunk's house and asked him about his moonshine making. Well, Spunk, he told him he didn't know what he was talking about. I guess Spunk got the message, and he and Dee, they packed up and left the county.

It seems that a lot of folks had fallen onto hard times and moved to Washington State. Their neighbors they were raised with, Charles Woods and his wife Nellie Mosteller Woods had already moved out there. When Spunk and Dee got to Washington, all the work that was to be had was either fishing or logging. Spunk, he took logging.

I guess most of the people who worked there was from the Tusquittee area, or were what the people out there called tar heels. Spunk, he worked there for a time. Then one day, Dee, she heard the whistle from the log train blowing and blowing and this was a sign that someone had been killed.

When the wives of the loggers heard this whistle they would all gather at the log yard to see who had been killed. This day it was Charles Woods. Dee said that she was there when the men came out of the woods, and she told Spunk it was time to go home. They packed their things and started back for Tusquittee. They made the trip and had gotten settled in for a little while, when word came from Washington that another local man was killed. This was Howard Ledford. He was from across the mountain over on Lick Log Creek.

Spunk, he and Dee, they moved back in the old house they had always lived in before moving. Before long, Dee, she was with child and they were the happiest couple on the creek. She said that they still had to work and make a living, and still barely made ends meet.

One day when she was about seven months along, she was carrying in firewood out behind the house, and fell and hit on her stomach. She went to the doctor but it was of no use; the little one, she didn't make it.

The neighbors back then, they would help with everything. The neighbors, Paul Mull—known then as Dommer—and Tuck Dowell and a couple more, they dug the grave and made the coffin. My grandmother Bertha Blankenship, she made the little girl an outfit which included a dress and a little bonnet and she dressed her for burial. They had the funeral the next day, and a sad one it was.

A few years later Spunk and Dee, they had another baby. This time it was a runny nosed little feller, and they named him Wayne.

Now, there is one thing that can be said about any of the Mostellers, and that is that there is not a lazy bone in their body; I have never known a lazy one of the bunch. Wayne, he lives on the family farm, and with his wife Nancy they raise cattle.

A while back I was driving up the creek and there was Nancy on a tractor racking hay for Wayne, who was putting it into round bales. Wayne and Nancy, they had a son whose name is Randy and he too is a hard worker. And a dam fine fellow who too has a son to carry on the family name. His name is Blake, and he is entering medical school to make a doctor. Now, that says something for the family genes.

Dee, she was telling me the other day that one of my cousins that works at the bank in Hayesville, wanted some bean seeds that were old-timey. Well, Dee, she takes some of them to her, and my cousin, she tries to pay her for them. Well, Dee, she says "Honey,

I was paid for these seed a long time ago by your Grandmother Bertha. Take them and good luck."

Sometimes it takes a while for things to come full circle but they always do because this is TUSQUITTEE where the people never forget a favor and the world's best moonshine is made still today. Or so it is said—I guess it's who you ask!

Frank Mosteller 'Spunks' Grandpa

Howard's Own Story

The year is 1979; I just turned 27 years old and was still wilder than ever. I have just come out of the woods where I was checking my crop. This has been a good year for growing with just enough rain and hot afternoons. In another few weeks it will be time for harvesting what few plants I have left after the thieves helped themselves.

When and if they come back, I left a little surprise for them. On my way to the patch I stepped on a copperhead; he was about three feet long. I caught the thing and went back to the house, I got me a fishing hook and line, and then I grabbed that copperhead by the head and put that hook in his tail. Needless to say, that was one pissed off snake.

I then turned around and started back to my patch. When I got there I tied that copperhead right in the middle of it. This might seem a little cruel, but after working all summer, well, desperate times call for desperate measures.

Two weeks later I went back to get my crop and most of it was still there. Of course the snake had been killed but not before he did his job. This is a sure fire way to find a not so honest person.

A couple of weeks have gone by and I have been working real hard. My girlfriend of about a year, she likes to have a few nice things. Today I came home at noon to get some tools I had forgotten. Well, I went to the house to check on her, and she had all of her clothes on the bed and said she was cleaning out the closet. I went back to work and when I got home she was gone; clothes and everything else was gone. I suppose she didn't get enough nice things.

Well, I did what every man would do. The next day when I got home from work my friend of many years was sitting on my front porch. We sat around for a little while, and she said she needed help loading a U-Haul for her sister who was moving to Washington State. I agreed to help the next afternoon, which was Friday. When we were finished loading the truck, I went back to the house.

In just a little while the phone started to ring. Well, it was my lady friend, Lynn P. We talked a few moments and she said "Do you want to drive this U-Haul to Washington with me and The Sheriff?"

The Sheriff's real name is Ronnie Killian and he's a good friend. Well, I thought for a good 20 seconds and told her it would take a good half hour before I could be ready.

Well, the plan was to meet at the By-Pass gas station at 10:00 that night and we would leave from there. I packed my clothes, which took a little while. At 10:00 we met at the station, and guess who was there but the county sheriff and his deputy! He was parked behind the car we were towing behind the U-Haul. We got out of the car and here he came and said we should take a little ride with them.

Well, Lynn and I crawled into his car and he drove toward where the stop light is now, (it wasn't there in '79). The Northwestern Bank was on the corner and they had a sign out in front. Well, the sheriff, he stopped in front of the bank and said "Do you know what that sign says?"

This sign said UNSPOILED CLAY COUNTY SELLS ITSELF. He could not have said it any plainer: get out and don't come back while I am in office. That was the start of an adventure that changed my life forever.

Ten o'clock that night the county sheriff dropped us off at the U-Haul. Ronnie, he started as first driver; Lynn and I, we sat back and enjoyed the ride. Now, that U-Haul, it didn't have but a 30 gallon fuel tank. We were towing a car so the gas mileage wasn't too good. We made Chattanooga, Tennessee where we filled up and change drivers. It was my turn now.

We made good time to Paducah, Kentucky. By the time we got there we were about out of gas. Well, we looked everywhere, and it being Sunday we could not find anything open. This truck was running on fumes and I knew we had to do something so we stopped at yet another gas station. It was closed.

I walked over to the water hose that was laying there and cut off about six feet. I then siphoned the gas out of the car we were towing and got the hell out of there. We had enough gas to make it to a station where we filled the truck as well as the car.

Well, we got on the road again and Ronnie was driving. We made St. Louis and the interstate 70. We were going down the road and Lynn and I were sleeping, getting ready for the night shift, when the truck weaving all over the road awakened me. I looked over at Ron and asked if he was ok. Well, he had a big grin on his face and said he was great.

A little ways down the road I awakened again. This time I told him to pull the truck over to the side of the road; he was drunk as a skunk. While we were sleeping he had drank a whole fifth of liquor and could barely walk. By the time we reached the Wyoming state line it was snowing real hard and there was no traffic. In a little while we found a motel and stopped for the night.

Three days and four bottles later we pulled into Longview, Washington and we were glad to be there; the trip had taken six days. After a short rest, I called my brother Henry who lived down the river 30 miles. A couple hours later we were on the way to his house on Puget Island. Well, I told Henry I was staying for two weeks and was going back home, but things didn't work out that way.

While there, his wife, she talked me into building them a house over on the mainland. Right off I could see why they needed a house; they had six kids and four bedrooms. Well, I started the house and a big one it was. This thing had six bedrooms and four baths.

On the weekends we would saw lumber for this house, and all week I would put it together. This was a slow process and a lot of hard work. Finally, after three months, we were ready for the roof. For this she wanted cedar shingles. Weekends we would go to the mountains and cut cedar into bolts and haul it to a friend's sawmill, and the next afternoon we would saw them into shingles. This went on for weeks.

Well, one Thursday afternoon we were finishing up loading the truck for the next day, when the owner of the mill, he asked me if I would like to work for a day. Now, I had been looking for work ever since I got there. I had borrowed 35 traps from a neighbor and had been catching muskrats, nutria (or coypu) and a few beaver. Every night after we finished working we would go around the island and spotlight raccoons. We were pretty good at it; we had killed 45 coons, 54 coypu (a large water rodent) and over a hundred muskrats.

I had sold these hides and the money was all but gone and I was down to four dollars. I was sure glad when Leroy offered me a day's work. Leroy, he said he only needed me for one day and be there at 6:00 the next morning. I was there at 5:30 and ready to go. When working in North Carolina I had logged for six years and thought

I had done it all. Boy was I ever wrong! Things in Washington are done on a very large scale.

The first morning we went to the woods, and when we pulled onto the landing I was a little awestruck because the logs were at least six feet higher than the truck. When Kevin Smith, the head faller, pulled out that chain saw I had never seen anything like it! This thing was huge and the bar was six feet long.

Well, Kevin, he started the thing up, and it sounded like an airplane. The first log was about 12 feet in diameter and 200 feet long. He sawed on that thing all day long and didn't get very far. Meanwhile, I was introduced to a 24- inch FRO. This is the tool that you use to split the blocks of cedar into bolts, along with a four pound mallet with a nylon head. That was possibly the longest day I ever spent in the woods working in my life.

At the end of the day we had loaded a flatbed truck. When we returned to the mill we unloaded the cedar onto pallets; we had cut four cords. Leroy, he paid me for the day of work. He gave me $100 and that was more money than I had made since arriving there.

He looked at me and said "Do you want to work full time for me?"

That was the beginning of a lifetime friendship.

At the end of the second week I was given the privilege of falling my first cedar tree. For this, Leroy, he picked out a small one of about eight feet in diameter. This was by far the biggest tree I had ever fell. The first was the easiest because of the flat ground it was on.

Well, from then on I was in on falling all of the trees. Sometimes I did the face, sometimes it was the final fall. Kevin, he was a master of the chain saw and it showed. He didn't back down from any of them, no matter what the size. As it turned out, every summer he went to Alaska to do commercial fishing for two months. Well, this put me as top faller for this time and with the responsibility of getting the wood to the mill. This time I was the one who got the new falling partner, a part time hand. Although he did no sawing, it sure helped to have someone to split the wood into bolts.

Well, several years passed and we went to the woods. Sometimes we had big trees and sometimes we had very big trees. One tree in particular comes to mind: it was 18'6" in diameter and on a very steep hillside; this was truly a giant and to stand in its shadow was truly awesome.

We set into cutting this giant and it was quite a chore. First we had to cut everything for 20 feet around it, and then cut two escape trails so we could get away from it in either direction. These trees were unpredictable; you never knew where they might fall. We first cut a face in the tree and what a face it was! It was big enough to lie down and sleep in. Next we would cut it from behind.

Well, this particular tree refused to fall because of the huge base. To help this thing fall, we had to use a large jack that would lift 30 tons. First we cut a notch for the jack, and then we inserted two steel plates, one on top and one on the bottom. This was the way to make the tree tip, and when this thing hit the ground it sounded like thunder.

I later found out that the average life span of an old growth timber faller was four and one half years. That's not a long time. In the four counties around where we worked, there was at least one fatal accident every week.

By now the house I was building for my brother was about done. I was living in a camper trailer for a year now. It was a three mile walk to work and I had been doing this for about a year. It was getting old getting up at 4:00 in the morning and taking a three mile walk to work. So, later in the week I moved my camper to the work site and this made it so easy.

The following weekend I was visiting my brother at his house on the island on Sunday morning, which was May 18, 1980. I had just poured myself a cup of coffee and was looking out the window at Mount St. Helens and the top just blew right off!

Now, it was 8:32 in the morning and by 9:00 it was dark. The ash from the mountain had blocked out the sun. For two days afterwards it never got daylight. When it finally did, the ash was everywhere, all over everything. We still worked in this stuff and it was no picnic. It took a couple years for it to rain away, and I was glad the final straw for me came in March of 1984.

We were working up Family Camp Road. I was cutting a windfall. Now, a windfall is a tree that has blown over in a storm, and this one was lying on a steep hillside. I had cut the top first as you are supposed to, and then worked my way to the stump. Now, this root wad was thirty feet high and you have to cut it off as close to the stump as possible. I had no problem with the top cut, the log was 14 feet at the stump; it is the bottom cut—and when the log breaks loose—when you have to worry.

I made the cut and was walking away with my saw, which weighed near about 80 pounds, when I heard Kevin holler "Run, Run!"

Well, I dropped my saw and started running as fast as I could, but it was hardly fast enough. That stump had rolled from behind the log and was coming fast. I was not faster. One of the roots hit me in the crack of the ass and knocked me about 30 feet to the side. When I looked around, that thing was going hell bent for leather down that mountain.

I got up and walked over to where my saw was laying—or I should say what was left of it—and only the tip of the bar was sticking out of the ground. I picked up what I could and it fit in my coat pocket. Up out of that hole I came and went straight to the boss. He asked where the saw was and I reached into my pocket and handed it to him. I then gave my two-week notice.

True to my word, in two weeks I was on my way back to North Carolina. I figured I had pushed my luck long enough. It had taken five years to figure it out, although that last incident took off several. When I saw Tusquittee the next time, I said every day the rest of my life will be gravy, and I was right. LIFE IS GOOD.

Boss Leroy Beard Finds a dry spot to watch

Cutting face cut in tree

Finished cutting 12' thru

Howard 2008 Utah

Howard and whole cabin

Howard on front porch of cabin

The First White Settler

There has always been a difference of opinion over who was the first non-Indian person to settle here. Some folks say it was the Moore family and some say that it was the Padgett family. I guess it depends on who you ask.

The Moore family was big around these parts, and the first one to come here in the valley was said to be a man by the name of John Covington Moore. He was originally from Rutherford County, N.C. He was born circa 1811, moved to Macon County when grown, and married a lady by name of Mary Bryson. For some reason they got it in their minds to move to the fertile and Indian populated Tusquittee Valley, so off they went with two horses loaded with household stuff and their first born, Little Bill. This was around 1833.

They crossed over Chunkie Gal Mountain which wasn't more than a narrow Indian Trail at that time. They made it all right and set up a homestead at a small Indian cabin they found deserted in the bottoms. Mr. Moore cleared some land to grow corn and started putting up a fence.

Along came an Indian—the one who's cabin he had homesteaded—who commenced to protest the goings on. This ended up in a physical fight; rumor has it that Mr. Moore almost bit the Indians thumb off, which caused him to retreat mighty quickly. The Indian later showed up with more red men and Mr. Moore had to get out his old flintlock to send them on their way. I guess he didn't have no more trouble then and they all ended up getting along.

When his crops were ready to store in his new garner, John took an extra horse and rode back to Macon County to buy more household equipment. An Indian woman by the name of Sally Peckerwood stayed with Mary and Little Bill. There is a street named Peckerwood off Cold Branch and I guess it's from the same family.

After loading his poor horse to capacity, he then headed back to Tusquittee via Chunkie Gal Mountain. At the end of the first day he found himself at the head of Tusquittee where he was able to spend the night with the Indian family of Yone Cannahut. (I wonder if the Indian he spent the night with was the one he shot at.) He got back home safe, and the land he had built on he later paid for during the land sale.

Years later, he sold his homestead and bought part of the Ford and Warne property at Brasstown. One day he was cutting a tree when his axe hit a rock and broke. When he looked to see what had busted his axe, he saw that it had gold in it! His lands later became the site of the Warne Gold Mines.

John C.'s brother, Captain W. P. Moore, is claimed as a Civil War hero in these here parts. He and his young bride Hattie Gash Moore moved into their new Tusquittee home in 1847 and raised six boys and four girls. A large family like that back then wasn't uncommon. Just about everyone had eight or ten kids; this was so everyone had plenty of help to raise food.

From the ten kids the Moore family raised, there is 250 descendents; a real fertile bunch I would say. I have visited most of the old cemeteries on Tusquittee and have found some descendents as early as 1777 at the Moss Cemetery.

Back to my opinion as to who was really the first white settler: Robert Henry. He was as tough as they came. He was born from Scotch Irish on February 10, 1765 in Tryon County, which became Mecklenburg County, now Gaston County. He fought in the Revolutionary War, at the Battle of Kings Mountain where he was wounded and glorified, and at Cowan's Ford of Catawba River, when General William Davidson was killed. He was one of the first settlers to come to the area which was to become Buncombe County, and he taught the first school in what was North Carolina west of the Blue Ridge.

Then he became a surveyor and surveyed a lot of the large boundaries in western North Carolina and Tennessee. In 1799, he helped in running the dividing line between the states of North Carolina and Tennessee from the southern border of Virginia to the Big Pigeon River.

In 1806 he was a solicitor of Buncombe County, which I guess means he was the main lawyer there. Bob Henry was also one of the first around here to start the tourist trade; he opened up and, for years ran the famous resort called Sulfur Springs near Asheville, later called Deaver Springs and then Carrier Springs.

On February 6, 1863 at the age of 98 he died in Tusquittee and was buried on Matlock Creek where he had lived for several years. We should all be thankful to him, because he wrote a lot of detailed accounts of the fights in the revolutionary war at King's Mountain and Cowan's Ford.

According to Dr. F.A. Sondley in his <u>A History of Buncombe County, N.C.</u>, when Bob Henry was just a lad, he was there on May 20, 1775 when the famous Mecklenburg Declaration of Independence was written. In his lifetime he had been hunter, pioneer, soldier, school teacher surveyor, lawyer, farmer, manufacturer, physician, hotel keeper, landlord, historian, author, politician, and frontiersman. This man was truly a giant among men.

Now, it seems to me that the ones that got the raw end of the deal was the Cherokee Indians. They were here for many years and called Tusquittee home until the white man came and screwed everything up. It seems that everything the white man touches just goes to crap.

When we were kids I went to Elf School. One day it was show and tell. Our neighbors the Cassadas (Tom and Ida) had a chicken that scratched an old flintlock pistol out of a decaying chestnut stump. He let me take this old pistol to school and show it. The gun was of Spanish origin and was probably lost or stolen by an Indian. At any rate, Desoto trekked near here back in 1540; this pistol was one that was lost or one of his men stayed with the Indians and lived. Also, when we were kids playing in the woods we found an old Spanish steel breastplate, or what was left of it.

This just goes to show that there was white people around here for a long time before the Moore's claim to have been here. The way it looks they were late comers. I guess it don't matter who was first; all most people want is to be immortal. Sorry folks, not in this lifetime. Some day folks will figure out that the only thing you leave behind is what you give away.

Moore House

Robert Henry at 94 years of age.

Event: Autograph 1837
Note:

Robert Henry's signature from an 1837 bond issued as part

of the administration of the estate of his brother, John Henry.

Event: Military Service Oct 1780 Kings Mountain, Lincoln Co., North
Carolina [2]
Event: Grave Marker

Robert Henry

Afterword

Robert Henry lived to the age of 98 and predicted his own time of death. He is buried on Matlock Creek on the head of Tusquittee. This man achieved what most men would only dream of doing.

John Covington Moore is also buried on Tusquittee and passed away in 1902 at the age of 92 and left 250 descendents behind him.

Alice Cothren was the best old lady I ever had the pleasure of knowing, and when she passed she was a little over 100. She left behind a very large family—in fact, several hundred descendents—some of which live here and a lot that live in the state of Washington.

Gene Cothren died in Cherokee county after having lived a long life and outlived three wives. He also had a full life in which he never hurt himself working, and his favorite pastime was hunting and fishing, and, of course, telling big tall tales.

Steve and Zadie Rowland, well, I don't know much about them now, but I do know that they raised a large family and both lived to a very old age and are both buried on Tusquittee.

Joe Blankenship died in 2004 and had a very good life and enjoyed every day of it. He also left four kids and a loving wife of 56 years. He loved to do farming and raise livestock; his favorite was hogs. There is no doubt as to where he is today for he was a God fearing man.

Muriel Blankenship still lives in the house that Joe built for her and still is in good health. She still likes to garden and raise her chickens, and still gets up at five a.m. every day, seven days a week. She also loves her grand and great grand children.

Smellit died at the age of 47 and we buried him next to his dad in a little cemetery on Rainbow Springs, which is on the Nantahala River. He enjoyed life to the fullest and loved to hunt and fish the river and did so every chance he got.

Chillie still lives on Tusquittee and I see him drive up Cold Branch every once in a while. He doesn't do a whole lot anymore since Fanny passed away. In the summer you can see him sitting on his porch and he will always wave.

Speedy Guffey still is living and in the same old log cabin he built for his wife Gail. He is wheelchair bound now and doesn't get out much, but on occasion he will go to town. His son Jessie and friend Shellie look in on him at least once a week.

Spunk and Dee still live in the same house and are doing fine, considering. Spunk has Alzheimer's and Dee, well, she has her hands full. However, she is making the best of it. She just turned 90 and going strong.

Tuck and Mettie are both gone now and spent their last days in the care center. Their son Louis lost the homestead to the county for the nursing home bill, but still comes back home every day and just sits and looks at where he used to live.

Ray and Mattie are still both living and just as in love as they ever was. They are still on the old home place and still raise cows and chickens along with their daughter Linda and her husband Jim.

Grandpa Will and Grandma Bertha are both passed on and it has been a long time.

The Sheriff has been passed on for several years and was still partying hard when he died. Maynard lives in Blairsville now and has been married for a lot of years.

Me and Tony are still friends and I see him all the time. He has a construction company and does all our work, and a fine job he does.

Randall and Ula May split up and a few years later he passed on. Ula May lives in Hayesville and is doing all right the last I heard.

Uncle Wade, well, we all know what happened to him.

Dewey and Gertrude are both passed now and their daughter lives in Washington State with her sister.

Uncle Bob Allison has been passed for a long time, and if I make any money with this book I am buying him a tombstone. All he has is a rock marking his grave.

The circle is as strong as it ever was, but is getting smaller every year. There is still no one else let in and I think they never will; however, the members are still all associated as when it was formed.

Moonshine still can be had if you look in the right place and know someone that trusts you, but it isn't as plentiful as it was once was— but is still as good!

The smoke is as plentiful as it was in the '70s and always will be, and as potent, I imagine. But you will have to ask someone who knows, because I don't smoke it any more.

Bear Paws and Turkey feet

Made in the USA
Columbia, SC
22 October 2017